LEARNING TO LEAD

Ten Stories for Principals

Michael Chirichello
Nancy Richmond

Rowman & Littlefield Education
Lanham, Maryland • Toronto • Plymouth, UK
2007

Published in the United States of America
by Rowman & Littlefield Education
A Division of Rowman & Littlefield Publishers, Inc.
A wholly owned subsidiary of The Rowman & Littlefield Publishing Group,
Inc.
4501 Forbes Boulevard, Suite 200, Lanham, Maryland 20706
www.rowmaneducation.com

Estover Road
Plymouth PL6 7PY
United Kingdom

British Library Cataloguing in Publication Information Available

Library of Congress Cataloging-in-Publication Data

Chirichello, Michael.
   Learning to lead : ten stories for principals / Michael Chirichello, Nancy
Richmond.
    p. cm.
   Includes bibliographical references.
   ISBN-13: 978-1-57886-528-4 (hardcover : alk. paper)
   ISBN-10: 1-57886-528-X (hardcover : alk. paper)
   ISBN-13: 978-1-57886-529-1 (pbk. : alk. paper)
   ISBN-10: 1-57886-529-8 (pbk. : alk. paper)
   1. School principals. 2. Educational leadership. I. Richmond, Nancy,
1945– II. Title.

LB2831.9.C45 2007
371.2'012—dc22

2006019788

∞™ The paper used in this publication meets the minimum requirements of
American National Standard for Information Sciences—Permanence of Paper
for Printed Library Materials, ANSI/NISO Z39.48-1992.
Manufactured in the United States of America.

Michael dedicates this book to his wife and mentor, Carol, to his daughters, Deborah and Teri, and to the school leaders who continue to inspire him.

Nancy dedicates this book to her supportive family: Harry, Dawn and Doug, Suzi and Wesley, Kate, Sara, and Caroline and to the next generation of school principals, who have an awesome and exciting opportunity to make a difference.

CONTENTS

INTRODUCTION

The principalship is more complex than ever. Principals are expected to supervise staff, discipline students, interact with parents, manage facilities, lead the instructional program, work on special projects assigned by the central office, ensure the safety of students and teachers, manage budgets, participate in schoolwide reform, build partnerships with social agencies in the community, and understand the legal implications of these diverse activities. Job descriptions often paint the picture that only a super principal need apply.

Principals must be knowledgeable about students, curriculum, teacher performance, and the community. They are expected to maintain an open climate and promote the values and beliefs that shape a school's culture. At the same time, principals are expected to manage day-to-day activities, which include scheduling, building repairs, supervising lunchrooms, and ordering supplies. Management activities often take time away from leadership. There is little time left in the hectic day-to-day schedule for the principal to engage in reflective thinking and proactive planning. Each day flies by without having enough time to lead.

Learning to Lead: Ten Stories for Principals develops 10 significant ideas about effective principal leadership. It is written for school principals, assistant principals, and educators who aspire to positions of school leadership. It is also intended to be a resource for those who are preparing the next generation of school principals: university professors and leaders of principal preparation programs. Finally, it is for those who love stories, who appreciate metaphors, who dream and imagine what leadership can be, and who are motivated to shape the future of our nation's schools.

Leadership is elusive. A beloved folktale of India tells the story of five blind men who want to see the prince's new elephant. Each man attempts to see the elephant in the only way that he can . . . with his hands! One man touches the tusk and compares the elephant to a sharp spear; the next man touches the leg and declares that an elephant is round and firm, like a tree trunk; the man who sees the elephant by touching its ear describes it as floppy, like a fan; the man who touches the elephant's trunk sees the elephant as long and round, like a snake; and the one who touches its tail thinks that the elephant must be a like a rope, thin and long. Which of the blind men sees the elephant? All of them and none of them, of course, for each of them has experienced but one small part of the elephant. So it is with school leadership. To see but one aspect of school leadership does not come close to describing and defining the principalship.

At times, school leaders must be decisive, solving problems and addressing issues quickly and deliberately. Other situations require school leaders to slow down a bit, communicate clearly, reflect, and remind others to keep their eyes on the school's vision, see the big picture. Effective school leaders take time to build trusting relationships and develop teams, while balancing the responsibilities of leadership in the fast-paced reality of a school. They are visible and accessible. Effective principals are willing to take risks and model courage for those around them. They see challenges as opportunities and welcome change. Effective principals recognize potential, nurture others, and share their wisdom. They carry on with calm strength, even in the face of a crisis or critical incident in the life of a school. In these roles, they begin to understand what the principalship is all about.

As difficult as it is to define leadership, principals intuitively know when it is there. Effective leadership is evident when it is experienced. This is not unlike the young boy who asks his father how he will know when a fish is biting on his line. The wise father advises, "You will know it when you feel it." Though difficult to describe, effective school leadership can be felt, seen, heard, and recognized when it is happening. Effective school leadership is illustrated in the individual and collective traits and qualities of the principal. This book is about the big ideas around which school leaders can develop traits and qualities to lead effectively.

Although many books have been written about school leadership, our unique approach illuminates the big ideas of effective school leadership through great stories, stories written for children. The lessons for school leaders portrayed in this book are distilled from the lessons learned through the characters in stories loved by young children. Consider Irene, a young Russian girl, whose story was told by William Steig in his book *Brave Irene*. Irene models for school leaders the quality of risk taking as she ventures out into the Russian winter blizzard to deliver a dress for the duchess to wear to the ball. Consider Appelemando, a little boy who loves to dream. In Patricia Polacco's book *Appelemando's Dreams*, we begin to understand how to get others to see and follow our dreams. Appelemando creates wonderful places that become the way of life for the villagers. His vision becomes reality. School leaders can learn the lesson from Appelemando and begin to understand how storytelling creates the opportunity to influence the thinking of their followers.

The literature written for and loved by children provides rich metaphors upon which school leaders can reflect and develop their capacity to lead effectively.

This book was born from our enduring passion for stories. The power and potential of the metaphor to teach in a way that will not be forgotten becomes evident throughout the chapters. Consider the musher who learns that he will need to live in the kennel with his sled dogs if the team is to achieve the goal of completing the Alaskan Iditarod. This teaches the importance of building trusting relationships in the schoolhouse. Think about the farmhand who knew that, to get through the crisis of a tornado, he would have to take care of the physical and emotional needs of the family. Managing a crisis is quite different from leading through a crisis in the life of a school.

We hope that you find the stories engaging and the metaphors meaningful. We invite you to take a journey with us into the wonderful world of dreams and imagination through children's literature. Discover the lessons that await the school leaders of today.

We wish to thank those who contributed to our work. First, we are deeply indebted to the authors and publishers who gave permission to use the stories that form the centerpiece of our work; next, to the library–media specialists who assisted in finding the right books for several of the chapters, Deborah Sparnon and Carol Kolenet, both of McKeown Elementary School in Hampton Township, New Jersey; to the graduates of the educational leadership program at William Paterson University in New Jersey who allowed us to use their case studies in several of the chapters, Beverly Belknap and Cindy DiDolci-Stockdale, Dawn Direnzo and Margy Leininger, Laurinda Marino and Chester Smitty Horton, Irene Cook and Frances Egan, and Mary Ann Cool and Cheryl Dunkiel-Berkowitz; to Lynn Liptak and Steve Mayer, extraordinary principals, who were willing to share their inspiring stories with us and thus enhance and enrich our work; and to the teachers and staff at two very special schools—Amsterdam School in Hillsborough, New Jersey, and Mill Lake School in Monroe, New Jersey—where one of us was principal. These schools were the setting for many of the stories that are woven throughout the book—these teachers carry the banner of excellence that made it a joy to be a principal. Special thanks to Rebecca Barajas, media specialist; Helene Williamson, reading specialist; Julie Staats, writing specialist; and MaryAnn Mullady, current principal, for finding great books to inspire us and much-needed words to encourage us.

OVERVIEW

After an extensive review of the current literature on leadership—leadership in general and school leadership in particular—we drafted a list of the big ideas perceived to be essential to effective leadership. We shared this list with professional colleagues, who eagerly argued that some were more critical, more essential than others. As we worked through the literature, spoke to people in schools, and reflected on our own experiences as principals, we embraced the following 10 big ideas of effective school leaders:

1. Leadership begins with a vision. Leaders tell stories about their vision; they inspire followers to embrace the vision; and they understand how to make their vision become reality.

2. Effective school leaders know the importance of building trusting relationships. They know that relationships grow and strengthen over time. They acknowledge that accessibility and proximity are essential to building relationships. Working and playing together become the glue that binds people together.

3. School leaders understand how groups become teams. They know how to communicate effectively and build consensus. They welcome diversity. Leaders know how to sustain the momentum and celebrate the success of highly effective teams.

4. Bold school leaders dare to look beneath the surface, through the lens of hope to see and nurture the potential in each student, teacher, and parent. They know the importance of nurturing the nurturers.

5. Strong school leaders are risk takers. They see problems as opportunities for improvement. Leaders who take risks model courage, and in so doing they encourage others to be risk takers as well.

6. School leaders focus on the need for change, more than the change itself. They understand how to take the journey from what is to what can be. Leaders know that the transition is more important than the destination.

7. School leaders have the capacity to lead with calm strength. During a crisis in the life of a school, leaders must model courage and attend to the needs of others. They look for the joy that can arise from pain, and they share it with others.

8. School leaders demonstrate respect for varying backgrounds and perspectives. They acknowledge that diversity enriches the life of the school. Creating a climate that moves beyond tolerance to acceptance is the goal of the effective school leader.

9. Wise school leaders know how to uncover subtle nuances in the day-to-day actions and reactions of those with whom they work. The wise leader is more like a musician in a small jazz ensemble than the conductor of an orchestra. The wise leader is always asking, What's so? So what? What's next?

10. The authentic school leader knows that who one is as person is who one is as leader. When you look at yourself in the mirror, is the reflection that you see the same as what others see? Can you accurately paint your self-portrait?

FORMAT OF THE BOOK

This book is reflective and practical. We crafted a format for each chapter, which includes the following:

Leadership Link: A clear and concise statement of the importance of each big idea.

The Story: A retelling of a children's story.

Lessons Learned: Lessons for school leaders that have been unpacked from the story.

A *Principal Reflects:* Reflections from school leaders that help to illuminate and illustrate the lessons; snapshots of situations that occurred in schools.

Connecting to the Leadership Standards: Case studies that connect to one of the standards developed by the Interstate School Leaders Licensure Consortium (ISLLC).

Tying It Together: Bringing it all together from the lessons learned.

Toolbox: A collection of practical ideas and activities for school leaders to implement in their day-to-day professional lives.

THE AUTHORS REFLECT

Collectively, we spent 64 years in public schools, including 34 years as principals. We lived through the joys and challenges of the principalship. We led our schools through the best of times and the worst of times. We laughed and cried with teachers, students, and parents. We were frustrated with the challenges and exhilarated by the successes. When we failed, we tried harder. We were touched by the humanness of school leadership and reminded of the need to walk the talk at all times. We learned that the principalship does not end when school is over—we found ourselves carrying the vision with us at all times, as we thought, reflected, considered, planned, and envisioned how magical a place our schools might be. We touched hundreds of lives, and we were recognized as being people centered. We went to teachers' weddings, kissed their babies, participated in students' funerals, and held parents close when they experienced the loss of a child. We learned the power of caring, trusting, playing, crying, and laughing together.

We do not have answers to all of the complex questions that school leaders face each day, but we have learned and grown because of our rich experiences and because of the people around us who supported our vision as leaders. We desire to share our knowledge with those who follow us. We share a passion for the next generation of school leaders. Our investment in the people who will lead schools well into the 21st century will bring a sense of closure to our lives' work to which we have dedicated our time and talents.

It is for all of this that we coauthored this book. We invite you to take this journey with us and look at the wonder of the principalship through the lens of children's literature.

1

COLORFUL DREAMS: CREATING YOUR VISION

A leader is someone who has the capacity to create a compelling vision that takes people to a new place, and to translate that vision into action. Leaders draw other people to them by enrolling them in their vision.—Warren Bennis, Author[1]

LEADERSHIP LINK 1

Leadership begins with a vision. Leaders tell stories about their vision; they inspire followers to embrace their vision; and they understand how to make their vision become reality.

> Sure enough, the villagers saw the dream. . . . They all followed this vision.
> . . . Never again would they question the importance of dreams. (Polacco, 1991, n.p.)*

THE STORY

Appelemando's Dream, by Patricia Polacco

Once upon a time, a boy named Appelemando lived in a village that was drab. However, Appelemando was a dreamer who had a vivid imagination. The villagers gave him the nickname *daydreamer.* He had a few friends who could actually see his dreams, which seemed to come out from the top of his head! Soon his dreams were captured on the walls of the village. The drab village was transformed into a rainbow of colors. The villagers rebelled and demanded that their children wash these dreams off the walls of the village. Appelemando and his friends were disappointed with the villagers. They walked away into the forest and eventually got lost. The villagers desperately began to search for their children. As they looked up into the sky, the villagers saw the bright colors of Appelemando's dreams. They followed the vision and never again questioned the importance of these dreams. Now the village is no longer drab. It is a wonderful place, a dreamy place, a place in which rainbows of happiness abound!

LESSONS LEARNED

Close your eyes and dream. Let your imagination run wild. Where do you want your school to be in 5 years? What does it look like, feel like, smell like, and sound like? How does it feel to meander throughout the building, gazing at the diversity in the faces of students and teachers? As you enter the learning centers, or what you may call *classrooms,* do you sense the excitement and joy of learning? Are students and teachers involved in the teaching–learning–assessment process? Is it difficult to distinguish between teaching and learning, learning and assessment, and teaching and assessment? Is your school community a place where leaders and learners believe in a common authentic vision? Or is your vision a hallucination? Like a traveler in the desert, is what you see only a mirage?

Vision building requires everyone to believe, to dream, to change. But change takes time. If you continue to shout about "my vision, my dream, my change," soon the followers will dull the leader's vision.

The craft in all of this is to create a collective culture in which the followers become leaders and embrace the vision, one person at a time. Patience and persistence are what you need.

Lesson 1: Dreaming the Day Away—Finding the Spaces

> There goes that slow Appelemando. . . . He'll never mount to much. He never does anything useful. He dreams the day away. (Polacco, 1991, n.p.)

Appelemando dreams the day away, but just dreaming is not enough. Vision building requires us to find spaces and flow through them, much like a stream that creates new pathways. When the resistance gets tougher, the stream knows how to go another way, gaining momentum with each and every turn. It's like that with vision building. People will resist. Not everyone will follow. Sometimes we must leave the resisters alone for a while as we go another way and pick up new momentum, new followers, and then go back to those who have chosen another pathway. Sometimes they will never follow. When that happens, continue to build a critical mass of followers. Soon they will overtake the inertia of the resisters. Eventually, the resisters will move out of the way, go away, or fade away.

> The one who hacks his way most quickly dulls himself. The one who carves his way lasts longer. The one who finds the spaces and flows through them, longest of all. (Herman, 1994, p. 76)

Lesson 2: Big Dreams, Tall Dreams, Little Dreams— It's All About Vision Acts

> Appelemando enjoyed dreaming just for them. He did big dreams. He did tall dreams. He did little dreams. He did middle dreams. (Polacco, 1991, n.p.)

Appelemando loved to dream. Leaders love to dream, too, and effective leaders learn to tell stories about their dreams. They inspire others to follow along. Leaders live their stories. They are engaged in acts of doing. Leaders must do what they say and say what they do. It's about being authentic. Leadership is about making a vision happen. It is what Lorraine Monroe (2001), founder and executive director of the School Leadership Academy in New York, called *vision acts*. The difference between a mission statement and a vision, according to Monroe, is making it happen. The essential focus is on the dream—how will we reach it? do we understand how it can become real? The leader is teacher. She makes the vision become reality by teaching followers about the dream.

When I introduced myself at a workshop a few years ago, I bragged that I was a teacher for 36 years, a principal for 17 years, and a professor for 5 years. Assuming that I began my professional career at the age of 22, I would be 80 years old. Someone shouted out from the audience, "You don't look 80." And she was correct!

I always considered myself a teacher. I was an elementary school teacher, a college teacher, and (as principal) the teacher of teachers, students, and parents. If we want to be a visionary leader, we must always be teacher and engage others in vision acts.

Lesson 3: Transformation—Frogs, Butterflies, and People

> "I'll find who is responsible for this prank," the mayor said, as he saw the crowd that had gathered. (Polacco, 1999, n.p.)

Appelemando transformed the village by the power of his dreams. However, the villagers did not like the changes, and the children did not understand how Appelemando's dream transformed their village. Leaders, however, understand how their vision is transformed into reality.

The tadpole becomes a frog, and the caterpillar is transformed into a splendid butterfly. Nature seems to understand the process better than we do. We struggle to understand the complexity of getting others to accept our vision, of making our vision real. Yet the process is simple—focus on the individual, inspire others, influence minds through storytelling, and create a culture of intellectual inquiry and reflective practitioners.[2]

> I lead a team of incoming plebes during basic training. I thought I had to lead the way that I saw others doing it—with stress and shouting, like a traditional drill sergeant. Well, my unit performed very badly. And they hated me. That experience shook me up. I realized that leadership isn't rule-based. It isn't about stress. It's about inspiration, about setting and communicating a vision. (Hammonds, 2001, p. 114)

Leaders influence and inspire followers by the stories they tell and the life they lead. What you do and how you speak are guided by your thinking. Your thinking is guided by your values and beliefs. If you really believe in your vision, it will begin to become evident through your actions and in your conversations. You will be recognized as an authentic leader, building from inside out (Evans, 1996). Picture your values, beliefs, talk, and behaviors as four large circles, somewhat distant from each other at first. As they begin to converge, you become more and more authentic. Followers are attracted to authentic leaders. You begin to create a synergy that influences and inspires followers. Your vision is now becoming *our* vision. You become more and more self-confident. You begin to take risks, push toward the edge.

Leaders tell stories about their vision. Like Appelemando's dreams, your stories will begin to influence the thinking of your followers. Your new story begins to take hold, to captivate followers, and a powerful vision emerges.[3]

Leaders are passionate about their stories. Passion ignites the flame in others. Followers begin to embrace the vision, and it begins to become reality.

Leaders focus on individuals, one person at a time. If followers are not accepting your vision, you support them. You are the leader who is always there.

As principal, you are one of many leaders in your school. When you understand this concept, others will begin to take risks and emerge as leaders. Followers become leaders. They become self-empowered to lead. The vision becomes their story. The vision lives on, and the cycle continues.

Transformation thrives in intellectual environments. Leaders learn, and learners lead. The school becomes a learning community. Collaboration is valued, and people work collegially to create healthy climates.[4] Leaders and learners understand the vision. They tell stories about the vision. Their conversations take on new meanings. The environment becomes risk-free, and the vision becomes reality.

Lesson 4: Vibrant and Dynamic Visions

> But the harder Appelemando tried to dream, the more impossible it became. Nothing came to his mind. (Polacco, 1991, n.p.)

Sometimes we try too hard. Our vision may seem impossible to achieve. Leaders must understand that visions cannot be forced on others. Visions must capture the imagination of followers and reshape their reality. Vision building takes time.

I once posed a question to the principal of an elementary school: "What is your vision for this school?" She replied, "Our vision is not visible. You will not find it displayed on the walls or in the classrooms. But ask any staff member about it, and they all know what it is. But tomorrow, it may be different than today."

Visions are vibrant and dynamic. They cannot be static. They are always becoming, emerging, evolving, transforming. A vision is not a destination. If it were, there would be no place to go once we get there.

Lesson 5: Celebrate and Dance Together

> Now the village is no longer a drab place. . . . It is a dreamy place. It is a wonderful place. (Polacco, 1991, n.p.)

When the dream became a reality, the villagers celebrated. Leaders, too, must not forget to celebrate successes. Celebrations create professional intimacy, and intimacy strengthens community. Celebrate your successes together.

When the artist completes her dance, her sculpture, or her song, the audience applauds. You, too, must applaud the successes of your staff.

You know that your vision is successful when others enter into the school and can sense, feel, see, hear, and understand the vision. Soon everyone recognizes the vision. Imagine entering an art gallery, looking at a wonderful painting, and recognizing the artist. Just as you recognize an artist's work, others must be able to recognize your vision when they enter the school. There is a voice in a vision, and everyone begins to hear it. More important, they begin to understand it. The vision has arrived!

The leader's challenge is to bring the vision into reality, to transform the vision from what can be to what is. Effective leaders have great visions, but they go a step further. Their visions become reality through the stories they tell and the relationships they develop. This reality strengthens and grows because great leaders inspire followers, focus on individuals, understand how to influence their thinking, and build communities of learners and leaders. A school with a vision will be a place where everyone will value lifelong learning.

Lesson 6: From Dream to Reality

> Bright colors of every hue, shape, and texture floated from the top of Appelemando's head. They twisted through the air. The wind caught them and lifted them above the trees. (Polacco, 1991, n.p.)

Appelemando understood the power of his dreams. The village prospered because the people believed in the power of his dreams. The dream became real.

A few years ago, my wife and I were passengers on a cruise ship that was headed toward Alaska. One evening we met Michael Modzelewski, author of *Inside Passage: Living With Killer Whales, Bald Eagles, and Kwakiutl Indians* (1991).[5] He left his home in Aspen, Colorado, for a deserted island in Blackfish Sound, in the Inside Passage, the rugged coastline between Seattle and Alaska. In his book, Michael wrote of why life assumes the reality of myths and dreams.

> The Inside Passage is real dream country. Even on land you are moved. The tides that carry the great whales move the bulk of your thoughts just as effortlessly. On the islands, the surrounding sea enters your thoughts just as effortlessly. On the islands, the surrounding sea enters your subconscious, creating a ripple mirror that reflects reality from many perspectives. There is no concrete or asphalt to fix attitudes, harden dreams. The world around constantly flows in many levels, swirling deep fathoms into you, loosening holdfasts and safeguards, stirring up sediment, provoking protean change.
>
> Now I understood why, to the Kwakiutls, life often assumed the reality of the myth. (p. 129)

The leader's vision creates a magic that will transform the world much like Appelemando's dreams transformed the village. Followers accept the vision because they trust the leaders. The power of visionary leadership lies in the authenticity of the leader.

A Final Lesson: Living Up to Your Part of the Bargain

Appelemando shared his dreams with the villagers, who initially rejected his unusual talent. He was accepted by his peers, but he still had to convince the villagers that his dreams had the power to transform the village from a drab place to one of wonderful color. To prove his point, Appelemando used his power to dream, and he saved the children who were lost with him in the forest. He did not let the villagers change his dreams. He always dreamed despite the pressure on him from the villagers to change—to become less of a dreamer, to stop painting dreams. Appelemando's dream was not their vision. They only knew the village as drab. But Appelemando traveled throughout the village, always sharing his dreams, which eventually transformed the village into a colorful, happy place. His relationship with the villagers became stronger. They finally embraced Appelemando's dreams. As he continued to develop these relationships, the villagers saw him as authentic—what he believed, he did. His behaviors were consistent with his beliefs.

Leaders must be authentic. They must do what they say and say what they do. If they do not live up to their part of the bargain, their vision will not happen.

CONNECTING TO THE LEADERSHIP STANDARDS: A CASE STUDY—SCHOOLS WITHIN A SCHOOL

City Center Regional High School is a large urban comprehensive high school that introduced the schools-within-a-school concept, but many parents, teachers, and students have been voicing concerns about this new approach. Incoming freshmen must select their school within a school when they complete their application for admission to City Center.[6]

Standard I

A school administrator is an educational leader who promotes the success of all students by facilitating the development, articulation, implementation, and stewardship of a vision of learning that is shared and supported by the school community.

City Center Regional High School is a comprehensive regional school with an enrollment of 1,000 students. Upon graduating eighth grade, students in four regional K–12 districts have an option to attend their local high schools or apply for admission to City Center. Students who are admitted must choose one of the schools within a school, beginning in ninth grade. They must continue in that school throughout their high school career. Previous to this year, entering freshmen experienced all 10 schools within a school throughout their freshmen year, in career tracts. They spent 15 days in each career tract and then chose their major tract at the end of the year.

The new vision for the schools-within-a-school concept eliminated the exploratory career tracts for freshmen and now allows for more intense, more focused career preparation that spans 4 years rather than 3 years. Each schools-within-a-school curriculum includes the required state core curriculum in addition to the special curriculum for that particular school.

This vision for the schools-within-a-school concept was developed by the principal, assistant principals, superintendents of the regional schools, and a small group of interested teachers. City Center has 10 career-related schools within a school. Because each school is small and team focused, this new vision for the high school provides opportunities for community building. The schools-within-a-school concept includes construction technology; automotive technology; landscape design; performing arts; culinary arts; and academies of information technology, business and finance, medical arts, criminal justice/public safety, and science/mathematics. Each of the 10 career-related schools has choices, or specialties. For example, a student in the School of Construction Technology can major in air conditioning/refrigeration, carpentry, plumbing, or residential/industrial electrical work.

The annual acceptance process is grueling for the 1,000 applications that are submitted for 300 openings. Many students are eager to attend City Central. They and their parents believe that it is safe and that it offers more options than do their district high schools. Because admission is so competitive, many students apply to the school in which they think they have the best chance of being admitted, rather than to the one in which they have the most interest.

Before changing to the schools-within-a-school concept, high school administrators and a small group of interested teachers spent a year studying and visiting other high schools that had similar structures.

Subsequently, the administrators determined that the schools-within-a-school concept was the best way to proceed, and they set out to present their vision to the staff and district community.

As this new vision about educating high school students began, not all staff bought into it. A majority of the staff thought that, when students rotated through all 10 career tracts, they would have more opportunities to learn about the alternatives. Teachers would have more opportunities to influence students in their choice of a career tract. Now, many teachers feared losing their jobs if not enough students signed up for their school within a school.

Recently, the principal had to meet with several parents whose children were eligible for special education. The discussions focused on the academic requirements for the more difficult academies, as compared to the requirements for the schools of construction technology, automotive technology, landscape design, performing arts, and culinary arts. Fewer special education students were admitted to the academies than were regular education students. Admission to the other five schools was equally divided between special and regular education students.

- Did the school leaders at City Central promote the success of all students by facilitating the development, articulation, implementation, and stewardship of a shared vision?
- How can the school leaders build a critical mass of staff and community members who will embrace this vision for learning?
- Examine the knowledge, dispositions, and performance indicators listed under Standard 1 (see Appendix). Which were lacking in the school leaders' plan and in the school leaders themselves as they developed this new vision for City Central?

TYING IT TOGETHER

- Resisters—usually 10% of a staff—can take up to 90% of the school leader's time. We must know when to leave the resisters alone and spend more time with the 90% of the staff who are waiting for us to move forward with them.
- Leaders are effective teachers.

- A leader who aspires to create a collective vision must focus on the individual, inspire others, influence minds through storytelling, and create a culture of intellectual inquiry and reflective practice.
- A vision is vibrant and dynamic. It is always becoming. One never quite arrives at a stop called *vision*. If we did, there would be no place to go afterward.
- Leaders have visions, not hallucinations. When they turn around, there are people following them.
- Followers will embrace the vision, but it takes time.

THE TOOLBOX: DEVELOPING A VISION

Nanus (2003) offered practical suggestions to develop a new vision for organizations.[7] He began by suggesting that a vision is a mental model of what can be and what we hope to achieve. Visions are idealistic; they are pictures of what the future can bring to us. They fit into the culture, history, and values that our staff embraces. Context is important to vision, and the first step in building a successful vision is knowing where you are and where you have been—that is, the history of the school. The vision inspires and clarifies direction and purpose. It sets ambitious goals.

Here is a process that will help shape the vision for your school: Engage in conversations about the vision with your audiences inside and outside the school. These informal conversations will begin to shape and reshape the vision. Include not only staff and students in your conversations but the community and parents, local residents, business people, and local government officials.

Keep an open mind. Remember, a vision begins to take on its unique shape, much like an amoeba. Your role as principal is to guide the vision and move it along as it becomes the dream of the school community. It's a collective vision. It's alright if it is not all your vision—and it shouldn't be!

Remember that vision building will result in change. Change takes time and causes turbulence. Expect it, embrace it, and throughout the turbulence keep focused on the vision.

Once the vision is understood and accepted by the school community, crafting a mission statement is essential. A mission statement explains the vision. The mission statement is the school's purpose, and the vision is its direction. Each school's vision and its mission statement should be unique.

Here is a process for developing a vision and a mission statement for your school: Bring together a group of representatives from your shareholders—teachers, parents, and other staff members. Consider including students if you are principal in a middle school or high school.

- First, ask several essential questions of everyone: What is the purpose of education and schooling? How does this affect your beliefs about what our school should be like? How does all of this fit into the district's mission statement? Allow time for each table group to have conversations about these questions.
- Next, ask each person to illustrate her vision for our school. This is what could be—your hopes, aspirations, and dreams. Give everyone time to complete the picture. Have paper and color markers or pens available.
- Reorganize the larger group into smaller, diverse groups of five or six. Define consensus. Ask each person to share her illustration with the others and reach consensus on a vision for our school.
- As they do this, ask the groups to identify the essential characteristics of their collective vision. List each characteristic. Try to limit the essential characteristics to no more than five.
- When the groups are finished, reconvene the participants. Ask each group to share the results of their conversations.
- Return to the smaller groups. Revisit the group's illustration of the vision and its essential characteristics. As a result of the conversations with the larger group, begin to change or modify the vision and its essential characteristics.
- Finally, come together again as one group. Continue your conversations and reach consensus on the school's vision and its essential characteristics.
- Discuss this vision with the entire staff, the parents, and other shareholders. Begin to tell the story and paint a vibrant picture. Give everyone time to accept or make suggestions for changing the vision. Over time, finalize the process though consensus building.

Table 1.1.   Assessment Chart for Mission Statement and Vision

Essential characteristics from our vision and our mission statement	What are we doing that supports this characteristic?	What do we need to do that will support this characteristic more?

- Once that is completed, begin the process again, but focus on developing the mission statement. The mission statement is the vision put into words. It should be brief, two or three sentences at most. The mission statement should contain each of the essential characteristics. It should be clear, focused, and written in language that the entire school community can understand. The mission statement should embody the core values of the vision. It should be powerful enough to inspire change—change from what is to what can be.

- When you have completed the school's vision and its mission statement, revisit them at least once a year. The process never ends. The school's vision and its mission statement are dynamic.

- Use Table 1.1 to assess how you are doing. Place the essential characteristics—the big ideas—from your school's vision and its mission statement into the first column. Look for what you are doing in your school that lends support to each characteristic. Place the evidence into the second column. Brainstorm what you can do to strengthen each characteristic. This activity will refocus the school community on its vision and its mission statement. It will result in changes as your journey continues toward your destination.

NOTES

1. Blaydes, J. *The Educator's Book of Quotes*, p. 137. Copyright 2003 by Corwin Press, Inc. Reprinted by Permission of Corwin Press, Inc. A Sage Publications Company.

2. These four *I*s are characteristics of transformational leadership. Additional information may be found in Bass and Avolio (1994).

3. Howard Gardner (1995) has written about great leaders who told great stories.

4. Organizational climate is discussed in Hoy and Hoy (2003).

5. Michael Modzelewski is a master storyteller who invites readers to abandon the safe life for one of adventure. He settled on a desolate island in the Inside Passage, the coastline between Seattle and Alaska. Michael's story is one of a man who learned about self through this exciting experience. Copyright *Inside Passage: Living with Killer Whales, Bald Eagles, and Kwakiutl Indians* by Michael Modzelewski, 1991, Adventures Unlimited, Seacrest Villas, 1810 New Palm Way, Suite 410, Boynton Beach, Florida, United States 33435 (used with permission).

6. Several case studies were adapted with permission from the work of graduate students at William Paterson University, New Jersey. Their names are listed in the introduction.

7. Nanus (2003) discussed these characteristics of a good vision, what vision is not, and how to get started with vision setting.

2

LIFE IN THE KENNEL:
BUILDING TRUSTING RELATIONSHIPS

Alone we can do so little; together we can do so much.—Helen Keller[1]

LEADERSHIP LINK 2

Effective school leaders know the importance of building trusting relationships. They know that relationships grow and strengthen over time. They acknowledge that accessibility and proximity are essential to building relationships. Working and playing together become the glue that binds people together.

THE STORY

"Becoming Dog," by Gary Paulsen*

I had camped with the dogs many times, and they had come to understand it as a way of life. First, they were tied to trees, then I lit a fire,

---

*Excerpt from *Winterdance*, copyright 1994 by Gary Paulsen, reprinted by permission of Harcourt, Inc.

fed them, then uncurled the bag in the sled or on foam pads or in the fall on a pile of leaves, and we all slept until morning, and it was daylight when we would go back to work.

This was radically different.

This was the kennel. I had never slept there before. When they were in the kennel—where each dog was on a chain and had its own house— I always went to the house and they went to their houses and we all slept until the next time we would see each other.

This time I didn't go away and it altered the way they saw me, felt about me, thought of me and my actions, and changed the way I thought as well—started me thinking right.

Started me thinking in terms of dog and not human.

It was a clear night; stars splattered across the sky in the brightness that can only come from the cold taking the humidity out of the air. Brilliant spots of light that seemed just over head high.

I considered where to sleep. The dogs whimpered a bit, and when it became clear that I wasn't going to feed or pet them they settled and sat and watched me. . . .

I settled next to Devil. There was no particular reason for it, other than the fact that the ground was level there, flat, and it seemed like a decent place to sleep. I put the foam pad down and the bag on top of it and shucked my coveralls and shoepacs and slid in. Next to me I arranged footgear and I poured a cup of tea from the thermos and propped up on one elbow to sip tea and look at the sky and the kennel, life, everything.

Devil was sitting directly in front of me, staring at me.

"Hi." It was just serendipity, a silliness, but he jumped like I'd screamed at him.

And his tail wagged.

It was the first time I'd seen his tail wag since he'd come to us and I smiled.

"How are you?"

Another wag. What the hell, I thought, he's being friendly. I reached out to pet him. The tail stopped wagging instantly and he growled, soft thunder, and I pulled my hand back. Another dog—I couldn't tell who— answered the growl and then a third and somebody (I thought Cookie) started a small song, just a night song, and they all joined in. I leaned my head back and joined, harmonizing the best I could—though still not as well as most of them could do it—and they didn't stop but kept singing and I kept singing with them for three or four minutes.

Whereupon they all stopped, suddenly, and caught me with a note hanging. I felt foolish and looked at Devil, who was still sitting there, watching me.

"I didn't know you were going to stop."

He wagged his tail, cocked his head, and looked at my face.

"I don't know things yet." An understatement that. "You guys will have to teach me . . ."

And I realized when I said it that I meant it. What I needed to learn only the dogs could teach me, and I'm not sure if it was then or later in the night when I awakened once to see them all still sitting, staring at me, that I decided what I had to do.

I had to sleep in the kennel. I had to be with the dogs all the time, learn from them all the time, know them all the time. More than sleep, I had to live in the kennel.

I had to in some way become a dog.[2]

LESSONS LEARNED

Gary Paulsen's passion for running dogs led him to enter his team in the Iditarod, the 1,180-mile sled dog race through the Alaskan wilderness. He and his motley team of sled dogs endured the wilds of weather, impossible terrain, and animal attacks to complete the race. In writing about this life-changing experience, Paulsen unwittingly created an adventure story that carries strong parallels to leadership. His account "Becoming Dog" speaks to the need for leaders to build relationships and earn and build trust.

The musher entered the kennel and slept there to build a relationship with the dogs. But why does a leader seek opportunities to build relationships? First of all, the leader who is deliberate about building relationships dignifies the importance and contribution of each member of the team. The team member thinks, "I must be important if he wants to be in a relationship with me. I must be worth something to him and to the team if he wants to know more about me and learn from

me and know how I am thinking." The second reason for building relationships is that, ultimately, the relationship built on trust and respect
will create team members who give more and feel better about their
contribution.

Leaders who acknowledge the value of community consciously work
to build unity, sense of purpose, and shared values among members of
the school. For a school to achieve a sense of community, each member's contribution must be valued and celebrated; each member must
invest in a shared, valued vision, and the building of trusted relationships must be a priority. So what lessons can school leaders learn from
the sled dogs and their musher?

Lesson 1: It's Not a One-Night Stand—
Relationships Develop Over Time

Our musher decided to spend a night in the kennel, and in so doing,
he discovered how important this routine would be to building a strong,
trusting, respectful relationship with the dogs. But he did not go back to
the cabin after the first night. He knew that he would have to make a
long-term commitment to life in the kennel if the collegiality and team
spirit he needed to finish the race were to be achieved—and he knew
that some nights would be better than others.

The leader who desires to nurture trusting, respectful relationships
within a school makes a long-term commitment, one that will see some
good days and some bad days, one that will be challenged, one that will
be vulnerable to changing conditions within the school, one that must
be deliberately addressed over months and years. Relationships between people do not become strong quickly, nor do they become strong
without pain as well as joy.

Time brings opportunity to a school community. The events that
come with the passing of time provide the ingredients for relationships.
Teachers have to know that they can count on you and that they can
trust you. This comes only when that has been put to the test. The new
principal cannot stand before his faculty and say, "You can trust me."
Trust has to evolve. It must be earned. It has to be experienced. It has
to be felt. It begins with small things first as teachers reach out and give
it a try. Then the word gets out that "the principal will support you . . .

you can trust this principal." The seeds of a trusting relationship are planted.

A Principal Reflects: Emily's Story—Building Trust

Emily was having a difficult time with her class this year, and she shared with me how difficult it was to manage this group of students. She was a skilled veteran teacher; she had a strong track record; and she was highly respected by the parents. Although I knew that she was not having her best year, I was not prepared for what I saw when I went in unannounced one afternoon to observe a math lesson. It was without a doubt the worse example of teaching I had ever observed, and it took all I had within me to stay in the classroom for the entire period. Students were calling out, asking questions about things unrelated to the lesson, and walking around the classroom when Emily was presenting new material, bickering with each other about something that had happened on the playground 40 minutes earlier. No one learned anything new during that 45-minute lesson except me, and that was that Emily was in trouble. I left a note on her desk: "Please stop by after school." That gave me about an hour to decide what I was going to do about Emily and this observation report.

Emily did stop in after school, and I asked her if she had time to sit down and talk. We closed the door.

"What did you think of today's lesson, Emily?" was my first question.

Her broken response was "It was horrible. You would be perfectly justified if you wrote it up as a failure."

We talked then about what was going on. At first, she wanted to think that this was just a difficult class, but exploring that idea yielded the realization that it was not the students as much as it was how Emily was handling them. She knew it; she just did not quite know how to accept it. Just when I thought that she would be defensive and justify her performance, she started to talk to me, and I listened . . . and we began to turn the corner. She shared that her best friend was dying of cancer and that she was trying to help her with her two young children. She shared with me that after September 11 her husband, who had been at the World Trade Center that morning, had lost his job and was suffering from depression. She had twins in college. Her son wanted to quit college and come home to help the family. It all came out as I listened. And I was reminded that it is impossible for us to separate the personal baggage from our days at school. "Do whatever you have to do about this," she ended. "I am not worthy to have these wonderful children in my class!"

"Emily, forget about the observation report. I can do that another time. Trust me when I tell you this—I am not looking to find problems with your teaching. I am here to help you be the best you can be. You are not feeling good about what is going on in your classroom, and I want to help you turn that around. Let's talk about what you need, personally and professionally, to get you back on track." Together we agreed that there were some things in her life that she could not change. "You can have control over what happens in your classroom. Let's tackle that."

We agreed that I would start spending time in Emily's classroom every day, informally, offering her suggestions about how to get on top of things. She knew that she needed help; she just had not been strong enough to make it happen. I helped her with some individual students who were challenging her, and we reorganized some of her routines and procedures. We got her back on track, and 6 weeks later, when I went back in for a formal visit, I saw the old Emily, who was a confident, effective teacher.

"Trust me, Emily, I just want to help you be the best you can be." That is the message I want to send each of my teachers, and that takes time. But when put to the test, I have to be worthy of their trust, and I have to put my words into practice. Emily responded well to the message that I was trying to send: "You are important enough to me that I want to have a relationship with you." It was one of the most important things I did that school year.

Building relationships takes time, sharing good times and challenging times together. It requires consistency between what you do and what you say. In time, the trust comes, and relationships are built.

Lesson 2: A Common Purpose—
Learning and Working Together

The dogs had an important job to do. The relationships that developed between dogs and musher were grounded in the job that they had before them—running the rigorous Iditarod. Teachers have an important job to do also. The foundation of relationships is the responsibility that the school family assumes, the responsibility to which each individual makes a commitment to learn.

Ants labor together and know the importance of working as a team. Honeybees work as colleagues, each one doing a job that is important to the life cycle of the hive—the scouts, which serve as lookouts in the field, to see where the good nectar might be; the fanners, which beat their wings during a hot day to circulate fresh air through the colony; the water carriers, which find sources of water in streams and lakes and bring back to the hive this important ingredient in the process; and the cappers, which seal the honeycomb in wax . . . the bees work hard together. They become a community committed to their mission.

The bees and the ants teach us a critical lesson. Principals must work hard to affirm teachers on their job performance. Principals give out little certificates, write notes, and leave stickers in plan books. Principals leave notes in the mailboxes complimenting teachers on a great bulletin board, and they tell teachers that they did a great job at a difficult parent conference. There is nothing more powerful in affirming and encouraging teachers than to tell them that they are doing a good job, that they are making a difference for kids.

Reflect on the process of observation, supervision, and evaluation. It has potential to affirm teachers and encourage them to be the best they can be. Working together for a common purpose builds relationships.

A Principal Reflects: Learning From a Colleague

I had been in to the gifted/talented classroom to observe a fourth-grade lesson on Marc Chagall. It was an outstanding lesson on using critical analysis and creative thinking skills. I have a rule about faculty meetings: "We have to learn something, and we have to have fun at every meeting." So I asked Jenny, our gifted/talented teacher, if she would teach a miniversion of the Chagall lesson to the faculty. She engaged her colleagues in analyzing a Chagall painting and synthesizing the symbolism in this amazing work. The teachers' response was one of enthusiasm and interest, and they saw Jenny in a completely new light—they had never really known what she did when she worked with their students.

Everyone learned something that day, and Jenny left feeling great about the affirmation from her colleagues.

Lesson 3: Being in the Kennel—
Accessibility and Proximity Build Relationships

It cost our musher something when he decided to live in the kennel. He gave up the comforts of the cabin; he gave up his privacy; he gave up his space. Although he could have been inside looking at maps or checking the weather report, he was with the dogs. But if he were in the cabin, he would not have been near the dogs; he would not have been able to listen to them; he would not have been accessible to them, and they would not have seen and smelled and touched him.

There is clearly a cost to the leader who wants to nurture respectful, trusting relationships—time, interruption, and loss of privacy and personal space. It will not be possible to earn the trust and respect of teachers if the principal is not accessible to them. Books have been written about managing time. During 3-day workshops, principals put their daily routines under the microscope to see what they are doing wrong and why they cannot get their work done. They organize their days to fit everything in, and they learn to limit their accessibility so that they can make efficient, planned use of their time. But leaders who are committed to building relationships will learn that time and privacy are compromised.

A Principal Reflects: Ellen's Story—
Being There at a Crucial Moment

It was June, and the days had started to get really crazy—more playground problems, last-minute plans for field day, distributing yearbooks, coping with hot days in a building that is not air-conditioned, finalizing class lists, reading and commenting on report cards. It would have been so tempting to close the door and try to get something done. Ellen poked her head in and asked, "Do you have a minute?" I have always been amused when someone says, "Do you have a minute?" (of course it will be more than a minute) or "Are you busy?" (never) or "Are you doing anything important?" (of course not!). But I saw in Ellen's face that she needed a minute, and I invited her to sit down.

"I may need to be out tomorrow." Ellen was 4 months pregnant, and I hoped that this was not about her pregnancy. "Are you okay?" I asked. "I'm very scared," she said. "The sonogram is showing signs of . . . Down's syndrome. My doctor wants me to meet with a specialist first thing tomorrow morning." Wow, heavy stuff.

"It's good to get with the best doctor you can find . . . be positive . . . don't panic . . . get as much information as you can . . . will Rob be able to go with you? . . . call me when you know anything."

The call came about noon the next day: "They are now seeing a second sign of Down's. I need to have an amniocentesis this afternoon, but I will be in tomorrow."

I was waiting for her when she arrived in the morning, "Are you sure you should be here today?"

"Yes, I would go crazy if I stayed home today. They will be calling me this afternoon. I will wait at school to get the call here." A long day for both of us. Respecting her wish for privacy, I felt a responsibility to stand by her. And I did literally stand by her when the call came. "Are you sure, are you sure the baby is okay, are you sure?" She flew into my arms crying, "Thank God, my baby is okay!"

I did not want to be involved in that problem, and I did not really have time for that. I had not planned to sit with Ellen for 2 hours that afternoon while she waited for the call, but I am so glad that I did. I am so glad that I was in the kennel that day. Ellen trusted me with her fear. She shed her tears of joy and relief on my shoulder. The report cards were read, the class lists got finished, and field day went off without a hitch . . . and a bond of trust and respect had been forged between Ellen and me. I am so glad that I was in the kennel that day.

Lesson 4: Work Hard—Play Hard

Cookie offered the first note of the song that would break the quietness of the clear, cold night. The other dogs joined in. And so, of course, our musher would become part of the song, lifting his head to the moon, mirroring the behavior of the dogs, joining in their night song—Musher and dogs playing together, making music together, and laughing together.

Just as working together builds relationships, so does playing together. When I hired a new teacher, I always said, "This is a great place to work if you like to work hard. But we also play hard here. You have to know how to have fun too." And we do play hard together.

A Principal Reflects: The Battle of the Bathrooms

Last summer, my secretary and I decided to decorate the office bathroom. We talked the custodian into giving it a fresh coat of buttercup paint. We put a flowered border up along with some posters. I draped a cloth over a school desk and placed a white wicker basket on it with hand lotion, static guard, and tissues. When the teachers arrived in September, they loved the new decor of the office bathroom: "Wow! This is nice—just as nice a home!"

At our October faculty meeting I kicked off the challenge of the "Battle of the Bathrooms!" "I have $25 for each wing. Use it to decorate your bathroom. There will be prizes. The winner will be announced at a special Valentine's Day breakfast: You gotta love your bathroom!"

Three of the four wings got busy and started working on their bathrooms. One wing did a Caribbean beach theme, painting the walls to look like a beach and hot-gluing shells all over them. The sink was decked with a grass skirt, and fish netting hung from the ceiling. Another wing went with an outhouse theme—bee hives, butterflies, flowers, and a rainbow made out of handprints. The gym wing did a sports theme, complete with a putting green, a basketball net over the trash can, and megaphones painted on the wall encouraging patrons to *Go! Go! Go!* The last wing went light on decorations, posting a simple sign that said ENJOY FINE AMENITIES AT OUR OTHER LOCATIONS! They got the "too busy to have fun" award and were glad to get it.

A Final Lesson: You Are Being Watched

Our musher recalled that he "looked at Devil, who was still sitting there, watching me. . . . I awakened once to see them all still sitting, staring at me." The dogs were watching to see if he meant it when he said, "I don't know things yet. . . . You guys will have to teach me."

As leaders, we are also watched. What we do speaks much more clearly, more loudly than what we say. Lesson from the dogs—never forget that you are being watched!

CONNECTING TO THE LEADERSHIP STANDARDS: A CASE STUDY—CHANGE AND A NEW PRINCIPAL

Facilitating change is a daunting challenge for a principal, especially a new principal who has not had time to build relationships with teachers and parents. The school community often embraces "the way we have always done it" philosophy while the new principal attempts to respond to the challenge of the superintendent and Board of Education, who say, "It's time for a change."

Standard 2

A school administrator is an educational leader who promotes the success for all students by advocating, nurturing, and sustaining a school culture and an instructional program conducive to student learning and staff professional growth.

Sandra Sullivan is the new principal of Woodlake High School. Woodlake is a suburban community with three elementary schools, one middle school, and one high school. The high school has an enrollment of 950 students. This is Sandra's first principalship; however, she brings 5 years of experience as a vice principal in a nearby high school, 6 years of experience teaching high school math, and 3 years of teaching eighth-grade math. She recently completed her doctoral work in educational leadership at the state university.

The community sees Woodlake High School as one that should be achieving better test scores. On this year's state test, 79% of the 11th graders were proficient or advanced proficient in literacy; however, in math only 62% were proficient or advanced proficient. Dr. Mason, superintendent of school, and the Board of Education believe that these test scores can and should be improved. They value Sandra's experience in math and hope to see her initiate some programs to put new life into the high school math curriculum. However, it is not Sandra's math background that is most valued by Dr. Mason. In Sandra's previous district, she served on a committee that successfully implemented a block-scheduling model that maximized time spent on math and science and implemented blocks of time for staff development. Dr. Mason is convinced that block scheduling will make a difference at Woodlake High

School. He told Sandra that he expects her to have block scheduling in place by the beginning of her second year at Woodlake.

Although Sandra is familiar with block scheduling and can easily implement such a program, she is sensing that the Woodlake High School faculty is somewhat set in their ways. They may be resistant to such a significant change. During informal conversations with teachers during her first summer on the job, she was told that *things are fine here*. "We had a lot of respect for Tim [the former principal] because he pretty much let us make our own decisions." In addition, she had a conversation with the union rep, who made a point to remind her that according to the teachers' contract, curriculum work and committee work cannot be done during teacher prep periods.

Sandra knows that change is not going to be easy at Woodlake High School; she also knows what Dr. Mason expects of her.

- Design a plan that will help Sandra build the relationships with her staff and result in their willingness to move forward with the significant change to block scheduling.
- What are her greatest challenges?
- What are the resources that she will need to implement the plan?
- Who should Sandra involve as she moves forward with this challenge?

TYING IT TOGETHER

Great leaders know the importance of building relationships. Building the capacity to nurture highly positive relationships in the school setting will be enhanced if the leader considers the following lessons:

- Relationships grow and strengthen over time. Building substantive relationships does not happen quickly.
- Learning and working together provides opportunities for relationships to grow and develop.
- Accessibility and proximity are critical ingredients in building positive relationships. In a school, the principal must be visible and accessible to teachers, students, and parents.

- Play together and have fun . . . the glue that bonds people together.
- School principals must remember their responsibility to set the tone in the school and establish a positive climate for learning. Don't ever forget that you are being watched. What you do speaks more loudly than what you say.

We have woven many little stories and activities through the pages of this chapter that principals can take and use in their own schools. Here are two more ideas that are easy to use and that go a long way to build relationships.

"All the Good Things" Activity

The "All the Good Things" activity is designed to maximize the power of peer compliments in building relationships. Before beginning it, you may want to read to your staff "All the Good Things," from *Chicken Soup for the Soul* (Canfield and Hansen, 1993).

- Distribute a list that includes the names of each staff member, teachers, custodians, secretaries, and lunch aides. Next to each name there is a blank space (see Table 2.1).
- Ask teachers to write one or two positive words about each person. Provide time and a quiet place for people to do this; play some classical music; sit with them and do it also.
- Collect the responses as people leave.

Table 2.1. List of Compliments

Names	Compliments

Marcia Wolfe
an excellent teacher!
fun to be with
a million laughs, always brightens my day
concerned about students
always willing to help when I am frazzled
loves her work
takes pride in what she does
flashy dresser, great earrings
takes new teachers under her wing
puts her family first—I can learn a lesson from that!
loves animals
I can count on her to spice up any party!
a good example for us all

Figure 2.1. Sample Compliment/Appreciation Sheet

- Now the work begins: Create one sheet for each person on the list. Copy all the positive descriptors offered by colleagues.
- Copy each one on colorful, decorated paper (see Figure 2.1).

You may want to do this at a June faculty meeting and work on them over the summer. In August enclose each person's compliment sheet in an envelope with the welcome-back letter. Send it to their homes so that their families can see what their professional colleagues think about them. You may find that many teachers will frame and hang their compliment sheets in their classrooms.

Decades Activity

Group your staff according to the decade in which they graduated from high school. Give each group a sheet of chart paper on which you have written the following categories:

- Fads
- Dress code
- Music
- Dance

- Thing to do on Friday night
- No-no's
- Heroes

Each group works together to decide on and record the responses in each category for their decade. Each decade group then shares its chart with the whole group. You can have a lot of fun with this. The groups may find some of the music that they loved from days gone by and start doing the jitterbug, twist, or electric slide! Especially interesting may be the responses to the section on the no-no's and the heroes. The group that graduated from high school in the 1960s may say that the no-no was to drink beer and the heroes were John F. Kennedy and Neil Armstrong. The 1990s group may say that Madonna was its hero and that the no-no was unprotected sex.

NOTES

1. Blaydes, J. *The Educator's Book of Quotes*, p. 112. Copyright 2003 by Corwin Press, Inc. Reprinted by Permission of Corwin Press, Inc. A Sage Publications Company.

③

THE HEN AND THE GEESE:
HIGHLY EFFECTIVE TEAMS

Coming together is a beginning. Staying together is a process. Working together is success.—Henry Ford[1]

LEADERSHIP LINK 3

School leaders understand how groups become teams. They know how to communicate effectively and build consensus. They welcome diversity. Leaders know how to sustain the momentum and celebrate the success of highly effective teams.

But the little red hen said, "All by myself I gathered the sticks, I built the fire, I mixed the cake. And all by myself I am going to eat it!" (Galdone, 1985, n.p.)°

THE STORY

The Little Red Hen, by Paul Galdone

Once upon a time, a cat, a dog, a mouse, and a little red hen lived together in a little house. The animals were lazy, so Little Red Hen did all the housework. One day while working in the garden, Little Red Hen found a few grains of wheat. When she asked who would plant the wheat, all the animals refused. So Little Red Hen decided to do the work herself. Not only did she plant the wheat, but she also watered the plants as they grew, and she weeded the garden. She cut the wheat, milled it, and made a delicious cake from the flour. The cat, dog, and mouse continued to be lazy until it was time to eat the cake. Suddenly, they had the energy to do that! However, Little Red Hen rightfully ate the entire cake herself, every last crumb. After that, whenever there was work to do around the house, Little Red Hen had three eager helpers.

LESSONS LEARNED

Little Red Hen tried to entice the dog, cat, and mouse to work alongside her, but she was not successful. Leaders also try to get followers to work alongside them, but oftentimes they are met with resistance. They wonder why others do not want to join in the group.

Most people find it easier to sit back, watch someone else do the work, and then jump in when it all comes together—just like the dog, cat, and mouse in the story. But, like the little red hen, leaders know that there is a lot to be done, so they just do it. They do not wait around for followers to join in. After all, there is so much on the leader's plate.

When the cake was finished and ready to be enjoyed by everyone, the dog, cat, and mouse wanted a piece. Not getting their way, they finally agreed to become eager helpers.

How do leaders attract followers to join a group, move from group to team, and collaboratively join in? Perhaps leaders can be inspired more by a flock of flying geese than by the little red hen. Look up. What do you see? A V-formation? What is that all about? Your journey through this chapter will help you understand how to move from *me* to *us* and from *group* to *team*.

Lesson 1: Recalcitrant Resisters or Eager Beavers— Moving From Group to Team

So the little red hen had to do all the housework. (Galdone, 1985, n.p.)

At first, no one wanted to help Little Red Hen, but in the end she had three eager beavers ready, willing, and able to work with her. Somehow, Little

Red Hen got a group of animals interested in becoming part of her team. All of this happened, however, after some turbulence in the household.

Schools run rampant with committees. We form committees to examine every process—curriculum development, student discipline, school safety, technology purchases, and more. It seems that everywhere you look, another committee is needed. Sometimes we even establish a committee to assess the value and purpose of the other committees!

When the members of the committee convene for the first time, they come together as a group of people. They sit around a table, and the leader, who is usually the principal, gets things started. Everyone waits for the leader to speak; to take charge; to tell the members of the committee what to do, when to do it, how they will reach agreement, and even who will take the minutes. Everyone is waiting for the person in charge to lay out all the details. Everyone wants to be included, yet everyone is dependent on the leader. It is usually a time during which everyone is polite, cordial, and agreeable. Disagreement is not common during this stage of the process. It is the calm before the storm.[2]

The group reaches a point where participation begins to increase, members begin to challenge the leader, and everyone begins to disagree. The calm gives way to turbulence. Individual members speak out and express their opinions. Conflicts begin to emerge.

Eventually, the turbulence gives way to calm. The group members coalesce, appreciate each other's talents, and respect their differences. Relationships strengthen, and the members agree about their common purpose—their vision and mission. They establish goals and examine alternatives that best meet these goals.

Finally, new leaders emerge. Sometimes it's *me*, and sometimes it's *you*. Everyone becomes focused on the goals. Relationships become collaborative. The group is beginning to become team. Compromise is the norm rather than winning or losing. Dependency gives way to independency. Everyone is eager to help. The recalcitrant resisters become eager beavers. The group becomes a team.

Lesson 2: Robins and Bluebirds or a Cockatiel— It Takes the Three Cs

"Who will cut this wheat?"

"Not I," said the cat.

"Not I," said the dog.

"Not I," said the mouse.

"Then I will," said the little red hen. And she did. (Galdone, 1985, n.p.)

Little Red Hen was not really listening to the cat, dog, and mouse. Simply replying "Then I will" showed that she only heard the "not I" but was not really understanding its meaning. She heard but did not listen. The group was not communicating.

Teams must communicate effectively. Members must know when to listen and when to speak. If you are really listening, then you are not thinking about what to say to the speaker while she is talking. You are thinking about what the other person is saying. Clear your mind; focus on the speaker; and really listen. Pause and think. Then speak.

However, be prepared to be misunderstood. Not everyone will hear what you say, and, if they do, they may not understand what you think you said. Why does this happen? Everyone has her own worldview, and perceptions are reality. Paraphrase or ask for clarifications often. Ask someone on the team what she understood by what you or someone else said. You need to check on understandings frequently if you are going to survive as team.

As principal of a K–6 elementary school and superintendent, I have facilitated workshops for school board members for more than three decades. A frequent topic of discussion is the board's role in the curriculum process. The very first question I ask at workshops is "What is curriculum?"

There are as many different replies as there are people in the room. Each one has her own perspective about curriculum. For some, it is a product, a guidebook, the subjects that are taught, the standards and indicators that are mandated by the state. For others, it is a process that begins with assessment and ends with evaluation. Some board members are focused on big ideas. Others imply that it's all in the curriculum guide anyway.

If we presupposed that everyone knew what curriculum meant, we could all be talking about something different. Take time to clarify, paraphrase, and define key concepts. Otherwise, you will not be communicating effectively.

Communication is the first *C*. It is a two-way street. What we say is as important as what we hear. Good speaking and listening result in constructive conversations. It is all about talking *with* others rather than talking *to* them.

Consensus is the second *C*. When teams want to make decisions, they should not necessarily take a vote and agree that the majority wins. If the team comprises 10 members, the majority (6 members) is only 20% more than a tie. If the power is with the people, then teams demand consensus.

Consensus is about sharing and accepting ideas. It is like brainstorming. It involves everyone's participating, listening, and, finally, accepting the team's decision. Consensus is not necessarily everyone's first choice, but it should not be anyone's last choice. On a scale from 1 to 5, often called the *Fist of Five*, each person has to accept the team's decision with a 3, 4, or 5. If someone holds up a closed fist or one or two fingers, the conversation must continue. Consensus means that everyone will support the team's decision.

Creative collaboration is the third *C*. Imagine that you and I meet together. You bring a robin to our meeting, and I bring a bluebird. When we leave the meeting, we walk out with a cockatiel. That's creative collaboration![3]

Teams know how to collaborate. Members respect and are willing to accept divergent viewpoints. They build on these divergent viewpoints and create new alternatives from the diverse perspectives. The new alternative may resemble the robin: It maintains some characteristics of the bluebird, but it really looks like a cockatiel.

Imagine the possibility of achieving dreams and aspirations that were never attainable to you on an individual basis.

Imagine thinking and working together with others who see and respond differently to the world than you do but whom you find endlessly curious, intriguing, and compelling.

Imagine participating in deeply spirited, generative conversations that result in new shared understandings, as well as in creating something that never existed before.

Imagine what it would be like to be part of a community of commitment, where learning and questions were more important than knowing and certainty.[4]

Lesson 3: Let's Build Our Home—
Understanding Collegiality and Community

> Once upon a time, a cat, a dog, a mouse, and a little red hen all lived to-
> gether in a cozy little house. (Galdone, 1985, n.p.)

Like Little Red Hen, who lived with the cat, dog, and mouse, school
leaders live with their staff for 6 or 7 hours a day. And, as shown by Little Red Hen's friends, simply living together does not create a community, nor does it create teams.

If a group wants to become team, it must have the capacity to build
collegiality within the context of a learning community. Collegiality de-
pends on establishing an environment in which everyone welcomes and
celebrates new ideas. The staff is willing to take risks because these new
ideas are encouraged. The organizational climate is open. The principal
is supportive, and the teachers are collegial. They have developed professional relationships with one another. There is a sense of professional
intimacy. The teachers enjoy working together because they all respect
one another. Teachers respect teachers; the principal respects teachers;
and the teachers respect the principal. If we work in a school with an
open climate, then collegiality flourishes. Groups can become highly effective teams.[5]

It is not just about relationships. It is also about structure. If the
school is organized into teams or units, the learning community has a
structure that promotes the very concept that it seeks to achieve.

A Principal Reflects

When I began my tenure as principal in a K–6 school, the organizational structure was not typical. Grades were arranged into units—K–2,
3–4, and 5–6. Special-subject teachers—music, art, physical education,
and speech—were their own unit. The teachers in each unit elected a
unit leader to convene and chair meetings, arrange for substitutes, and
support colleagues when problems emerged. The unit leaders met with
me twice a month from 3 p.m to 5 p.m. This leadership team made
schoolwide decisions through consensus. The school's structure pro-
moted the concept of team. The picture of leadership in this school was
one of intersecting circles rather than lines and boxes. During my 13

years as principal, the unit structure prevailed, and the learning community flourished.

The principal must create opportunities for teachers to lead. The principal's role as teacher and collaborator becomes obvious when the structure is built around units or teams. The principal has opportunities to nurture teacher leaders.

Lesson 4: The Spider's Web—
Understanding Collective Leadership

> When the oven was hot, she poured the cake batter into a shining pan and put it in the oven. (Galdone, 1985, n.p.)

Little Red Hen knew that if she wanted to bake a sumptuous cake, she had to gather sticks for the oven, mix the right ingredients, and then let the batter bake for the right amount of time and at the right temperature. She knew that a delicious cake does not just happen. The cook follows a recipe.

Teams do not just happen either. The recipe to build highly effective teams begins with mixing the right ingredients. Leaders must have a deeper understanding about team building than they may realize.

First, leaders must understand the importance of building trusting relationships with others. They must understand how to sustain and strengthen those relationships, even rebuild them at times. We live in a world that is rich in relationships, with patterns that connect rather than separate. Our universe supports systems and interrelationships. Nothing lives alone. The world is a web of relationships. Like the spider's web, each thread is connected to the whole. If one thread is broken, the web loses its strength. "[The spider] reweaves it, using the silken relationships that are already there, creating stronger connections across the weakened spaces" (Wheatley, 1999, p. 145).[6]

Principals must weave a web of relationships within the school. Each thread is dependent on all the other threads. If one thread is broken or ripped apart, the web begins to lose its resiliency.

Second, leaders must understand their role and responsibilities. This will occur if the principal and teachers discard individualism and isolationism. Leaders must create a culture in which everyone is accountable. Teachers must be accountable for students, themselves, and one another. Principals must be willing to give up control and power. They must intuitively know when to lead, when to follow, and when to get out of the way. When everyone is accountable, when collectivism overpowers isolationism, a community that values caring begins to take shape. Collective leadership begins to emerge.

Third, in schools that embrace collective leadership,[7] everyone who looks through the lens sees the vision and speaks about the mission. That vision includes the teachers and the principal working together as experts, educational leaders, critical friends, facilitators, and coaches. No one stands alone.

In schools that nurture trusting relationships, site-based leadership teams replace site-based management teams. In schools where collective leadership is evident, everyone values caring, accountability, and collaboration. Collective leadership begins to emerge when groups become highly effective teams.

Lesson 5: The Fish Market—Sustaining the Momentum

> After that, whenever there was work to be done, the little red hen had three very eager helpers. (Galdone, 1985, n.p.)

The cat, dog, and mouse became eager helpers, but how long will it be before they drift away and snooze all day? How can Little Red Hen sustain the momentum of her team? Let's turn to a fishy story to find out.

A Principal Reflects

It was a sunny day in Seattle when my wife, Carol, and I decided to take a walk to the market. We had one day left before we embarked on our vacation cruise to Alaska from this port city. When we arrived at the market and began to browse, I could not help but hear loud noises coming from the end of the aisle. I looked down the aisle and noticed a crowd of people gathered around what looked like a fish market. The shouting, laughing, smiling, and fish flying in the air made us want to rush over to see what was happening. We discovered the world famous Pike Place Fish Market. It's the fish company that everyone talks about.

Pike Place offers fresh fish and something more—its employees are dedicated to having fun and creating excitement while they work.[8]

Employees at Pike Place Fish Market are not customer centered; they are people centered. You do not have to be a customer to get attention here. The employees are a team, working together to serve their customers. They want people to have fun and feel appreciated whether they buy fish or not. They understand how to sustain their momentum. They have a great attitude. Each employee looks at life as an opportunity, full of wonder, excitement, and fun. They sell fish but, more important, they sell fun. They are constantly in your face. Their mission is obvious—through their work, they improve the quality of life for others. They are committed to this belief. It's what they do. They are product focused, but they are also people focused.

If teams want to sustain the momentum, their members will join with the employees from Pike Place Fish Market and choose their attitude, have fun, and get in each other's face.

Lesson 6: Dysfunctional Teams—The Way Not to Go

The Little Red Hen is a story about a dysfunctional team.[9] What happened? Just as we can move from groups to teams, the reverse is true. Teams can become dysfunctional groups of people who no longer sustain their momentum. If the team members are no longer able to stick by one another, to have a sense of commitment to a common goal or purpose, then the team will unravel into a bunch of loose, entangled threads. The culture of accountability disappears, and blame predominates. It's *he did* and *she did* all over again. Ideas are criticized more than celebrated.

Members come to the table with hidden agendas. What you hear is not what was meant.

Groupthink causes dysfunctional teams. Everyone begins to become a *yes* person. Ideas are no longer a result of an individual's creativity. Members do not really say what they think. Even though there may be diversity among team members in their backgrounds, ideas, and perspectives, they become a cloth of one color rather than a tapestry of many colors.

The glue that holds teams together is trust. Trust is essential to sustain the relationships that move individuals from groups to teams to highly effective teams. Trusting relationships build effective teams, and teams build trusting relationships. Collectively, team members can sustain and strengthen trusting relationships. This relationship is transactional. The more that each member of the team trusts the other members, the more that other members will trust the individual members. Trust creates a sense of freedom to try out new ideas, to create a risk-free environment.

In risk-free environments, members respect one another's ideas. Respect strengthens trust. It is only through mutual respect that teams will be effective throughout their life cycle.[10]

Dysfunctional teams are scattered. Highly effective teams are focused on their goals. Dysfunctional teams lack trusting relationships. Highly effective teams value trust and respect. Dysfunctional teams take themselves too seriously. Highly effective teams are creative and playful. Dysfunctional teams do not take risks. Dysfunctional teams are not what leaders want or need.

A Final Lesson: Highly Effective Teams

The story of *The Little Red Hen* may not be the way to build highly effective teams. Just asking others to help will not work. Teams do not just happen. The leader must create both the climate and the structure in which teams can flourish. Once that happens, we are ready to spin the web. Each thread is carefully connected to the other threads. Relationships hold the threads together. Trusting relationships get groups to become teams. Once we get there, we must sustain the momentum. The cycle of team building is a never-ending spinning of new threads to reinforce and repair the broken threads. The spider's web is the way to go.

CONNECTING TO THE LEADERSHIP STANDARDS: A CASE STUDY—WORKING TOGETHER IN A DIVERSE COMMUNITY: A PLAN FOR ACTION NOW

Jonesville High School is located in a suburban, middle- to upper-class district. During the last 5 years, there have been significant changes in the district's school-age population. As a result, some significant problems related to the diverse student body have emerged.

Standard 4

A school administrator is an educational leader who promotes the success of all students by collaborating with families and community members, responding to diverse community interests and needs, and mobilizing community resources.

During the last 5 years, there has been a significant increase in the Hispanic school-age population in this suburban school district. This has changed the complexion of the high school. At the same time, racial tensions in the community have been mounting and have reached a critical stage. Hispanics have moved into areas that were previously inhabited by the African American population. Stores that once served the needs of the African American community are now are owned by Hispanics. There is animosity among the students in the high school, emanating from the tensions in the community. Eight hundred students are enrolled in this high school this year, as compared to 1,000 5 years ago. Sixty percent of the students are White; 25% are Hispanic; 10% are African American; and 5% are Asian, compared to 75%, 5%, 15%, and 5%, respectively, 5 years ago. The students hang out with their own ethnic groups. Whites do not usually associate with the non-White students. In the past 2 years, school records indicate that there have been numerous altercations among the groups. This has given rise to the gang mentality that has become evident in the high school and the community. Recently, two students have resorted to carrying weapons into school and have been threatening to use them against other students. The new principal and her staff want to develop a plan of action that respects diversity and promotes civility. She has interviewed students, parents, and staff. As a result, the principal has learned that the tension has been mounting. White flight has begun; racial slurs continue to appear in the hallways and on bathroom walls; and metal detectors were installed at the entranceways a month before her arrival.

"The Hispanics are taking over our neighborhood" seems to be the mantra of the African American and White students. More and more parents who are of middle to high socioeconomic status—Black, Asian, and White—are enrolling their children in private schools. The last three school district budgets have been defeated. Before that, budgets were always approved by the voting public.

As a result of the defeated budgets, cuts have been made to programs, and more and more support staff positions are being eliminated. The school leadership team has remained at the staffing levels of 5 years ago. The high school has a principal, two assistant principals, a director of guidance and special services, and five academic chairs. The most recent budget reductions for the current school year have included the elimination of five after-school clubs, three sports teams, and five staff members whose primary responsibility was to work with students who need basic-skills support. The positions were included in the cuts despite the fact that this school is not making the required adequate yearly progress to comply with the requirements of the No Child Left Behind legislation. The time for action becomes more pressing as each day passes.

- Identify three key issues that the principal must address.
- Design a plan of action for each of the identified issues that incorporates a team approach.
- How can the principal promote the success of all students as she tries to respond to diverse community interests and needs?

TYING IT TOGETHER

> Let us turn our focus away from the little red hen and toward a flock of geese. The lessons from *The Native American Voice* embody the power of TEAM. As you look at a flock of geese soaring in the sky, think of TEAM. . . . Together Everyone Achieves More.
>
> "Lessons From the Geese," *The Native American Voice*[11]

- As each bird flaps its wings, it creates an uplift for others behind it. There is 71% more flying range in V-formation than in flying alone.
- *Lesson:* People who share a common direction and a sense of common purpose can get to their destination quicker.
- Whenever a goose flies out of formation, it quickly feels the drag and tries to get back into position.

- *Lesson:* It's harder to do something alone than together.
- When the lead goose gets tired, it rotates back into formation and another goose flies at the head.
- *Lesson:* Shared leadership and interdependence give us each a chance to lead, as well as opportunities to rest.
- The geese in formation honk from behind to encourage those up front to keep up their speed.
- *Lesson:* We need to make sure our honking is encouraging and not discouraging.
- When a goose gets sick or wounded and falls, two geese fall out and stay with it until it revives or dies. Then they catch up or join another flock.
- *Lesson:* Stand by your colleagues in difficult times as well as in good times.

THE TOOLBOX: TEN STEPS TO SUCCESS

Who does not need a committee? We often abuse this structure by convening a group of people to give us feedback on a process, question, new policy, or critical issue, but then we massage the results. Committees are often advisory with no binding power to make decisions. How can we move away from advisory committees and begin to think about working with decision-making teams? How can principals create an environment in which collective leadership flourishes?

Get a group of people together. Yes, it is a group for now. Follow the one-pie rule—your tantalizing favorite dessert pie should be enough to satisfy the group. Sometimes we are off and running with too many people in the first place. Effective teams are usually limited to six or eight participants.

Lead the group at its first meeting. Establish a start time and a stop time. Ask someone to be the observer who will record some of what is happening. You could create a series of questions for that person, or she or he could just take some open-ended notes on the process that transpires.

Step 1. Be clear about the team's focus. What do you want to accomplish so that you will know when the work of the team is completed? That determines the life cycle of team. For example, if I am looking to make curriculum changes in math (focus), what changes will the team recommend to the staff? When that is completed, the work of the team is finished.

Step 2. Assess the environment before bringing the members of the team together. What is the school's capacity for collaboration? Is the context ripe for collaboration, or do I have to initiate some processes to encourage collaboration? Do the members work together in formal and informal settings, or is the environment one in which it is all about *me* rather than *we*?

Step 3. What are the assumptions that underlie the team's focus? In the case of the math team, are we looking to change the texts or the curriculum guide or both? Will there be parent, staff, and districtwide involvement? Will there be support for the team's decisions? What impact will state standards have on our work? How will this affect our adequate yearly progress for No Child Left Behind? What does the current research say about math? You must spend time on the assumptions before the next step in the process.

Step 4. Analyze the focus.

- *What's so?* What is happening now in the math program? How are most teachers implementing the current programs and curriculum?
- *So what?* What implications does the work that we do have for our students and us? Why do we do what we do in the first place?
- *What's next?* As a result of our discussions, what becomes important and urgent, important but less urgent, and not important or urgent? This prioritizes the team's work.[12]

Step 5. When you complete your conversations on these questions, establish your objectives. What do you hope to achieve as a result of implementing the team's recommendations? What is urgent and important? For the math team, this may be to improve student outcomes in math skills on the annual math assessments—state testing, authentic work defined by rubrics, and report card grades.

Step 6. Identify the best alternatives to achieve the objective. First, brainstorm ideas, then break into miniteams; discuss the best of the solutions that the team has selected, and then report back to the full team. Become critical friends during this process. Refine, refine, refine. The strongest solutions become evident over time. Less is more. Limit your alternatives so that your objectives will be achieved.

Step 7. Reach consensus on the team's work. All agree that the proposed recommendations can be supported by each member of the team to the larger audience—staff, parents, board of education, and superintendent.

Step 8. Develop an action plan for spreading the news. Who will do what? When will it happen? How will we know that we are successful or not successful? This is not about implementing the recommendations yet; rather, it is about getting others to buy into the team's recommendations.

Step 9. Regroup and reassess. Where are you? What survived? What has to be reshaped, thrown away, or strengthened in your plan? After all of this, the next step is for the school leader to support the outcomes and plan for the implementation of the team's recommendations.

Step 10. Celebrate. Teams should have fun and enjoy celebrating their success. Take some time to laugh a little, cry a little, and smile a long time!

- What happened to the observer? After the first meeting, take turns observing and debriefing the process. It may not be necessary to do this at every meeting, but do it regularly. Remember, the observer listens and does not participate in the conversation.
- Remember the one-pie rule? There is another rule to remember. It's the 2-hour rule. No meeting should be more than 2 hours. If you can limit meetings to 1 hour, so much the better. Remember, teams can distribute the work among their members, work in miniteams, and then return to share their outcomes. It is all about collective leadership.

Ten steps to success!

NOTES

1. Blaydes, J. *The Educator's Book of Quotes*, p. 139. Copyright 2003 by Corwin Press, Inc. Reprinted by Permission of Corwin Press, Inc. A Sage Publications Company.

2. Susan Wheelan (1999) discussed the four stages during which a group of people can become highly effective teams—navigating, surviving, reorganizing, and sustaining.

3. The concept of creative collaboration is discussed in Robert Hargrove's *Mastering the Art of Creative Collaboration* (1998).

4. Robert Hargrove (1998). *Mastering the Art of Creative Collaboration.* New York: BusinessWeek Books, McGraw Hill, p. 1. Reproduced with permission from The McGraw-Hill Companies.

5. The Collegiality Index (McEwan, 1997) is a useful process to assess your school's capacity for collegiality.

6. Margaret Wheatley (1999) discussed how leadership is more like the new science, rich in potential for new possibilities. New scientific discoveries are changing our understanding of how the world works.

7. The concept of collective leadership is explained in "Reinventing the Principalship: From Centrist to Collective Leadership" (Chirichello, 2002). The recent research of André Martin, Cynthia McCauley, Phil Wilburn, Allan Calaro, and Christopher Ernst (2006) supports the movement away from leadership as a position to a collective perspective of leadership as a process.

8. You can visit Pike Place Fish Market on the web, at http://www .pikeplacefish.com/default.htm.

9. An analysis of what makes teams work effectively and ineffectively is described in Lencioni (2002). Lencione highlighted five attrbutes of dysfunctional teams: absence of trust, fear of conflict, lack of commitment, avoidance of accountability, and inattention to results.

10. Sara Lawrence-Lightfoot's text on respect (2000) highlighted the importance of this quality in the lives of leaders.

11. This poem was written in 1972, to be used in a layman's Sunday talk given in the Northminister Presbyterian Church in Reisterstown, Maryland, by Robert McNeish. Used with permission from Robert McNeish.

12. Stephen Covey (1989) discussed the third habit of highly successful people, "Put first things first."

4

THE PATIENT GARDENER: NURTURING POTENTIAL

In everyone's life, at some time our inner fire goes out. It is then burst into flame by an encounter with another human being. We should all be thankful for those people who rekindle the inner spirit.—Albert Schweitzer[1]

LEADERSHIP LINK 4

Bold school leaders dare to look beneath the surface, through the lens of hope, to see and nurture the potential in each student, teacher, and parent. They know the importance of nurturing the nurturers.

THE STORY

Mr. Lincoln's Way, by Patricia Polacco*

The boys and girls thought Mr. Lincoln was a really cool principal because he wore cool clothes, had a cool smile, and did cool things. All of the students loved and respected Mr. Lincoln . . . all except one, Eugene Esterhause. "Mean Gene" was a bully, he always seemed angry; he picked on kids, and called people names. But Mr. Lincoln said, "He's not a bad boy, really. Only troubled."

One day, Eugene got angry and called Mr. Lincoln the "n-name." That was the day Mr. Lincoln decided he had to find a way to help Eugene become the person he knew this student could be. Mr. Lincoln noticed that Eugene liked to look out the window into the beautiful new atrium of the school and watch the birds. Mr. Lincoln noticed that Eugene liked birds and so he gave him a book about birds. He was delighted when he noticed that Eugene carried the book everywhere he went!

Mr. Lincoln asked Eugene to help him fix up the school's atrium in a way that would attract more birds. Together they planted shrubs and plants, scattered grain and seeds for the birds, and even built three bird feeders together. And the birds came! All of the students were happy and excited about the birds in the atrium, especially Eugene. As a matter of fact, Eugene seemed to change. He was no longer mean to the other students.

But that didn't last for long. One day when Eugene got into a fight at school he was brought to Mr. Lincoln's office. Eugene told his principal that his father had gotten mad at him for coming home late on the days he stayed to help Mr. Lincoln in the atrium. He told Mr. Lincoln that his father didn't like the principal because he "wasn't our kind." Realizing that Eugene's father was teaching him to be intolerant of other people, Mr. Lincoln took this opportunity to talk to Eugene about the potential in each person to be something great. He asked Eugene to promise to be the kind and tolerant person he knew he could be.

When a pair of mallards made a nest in the atrium and the eggs hatched, Eugene had a chance to prove himself. He found a way to lead the ducks through the school and out to the pond so they wouldn't be trapped in the atrium. When Mr. Lincoln complimented Eugene on the good thing that he had done, Eugene said "Hey, you showed me the way out, Mr. Lincoln." Then he stopped and made one more promise to his principal and friend, "I'll make you proud of me, Mr. Lincoln. I promise." And he did! Eugene Esterhause became a fourth-grade teacher and called his students "my little birds."

LESSONS LEARNED

The gardener nurtures the potential of the tiny seed to grow into a beautiful flower or a delicious piece of fruit. The sculptor looks at the piece of granite and envisions how it will become a statue. The kindergarten teacher looks at the young students and sees the citizens of tomorrow—doctors, plumbers, teachers, astronauts, and electricians. When one is in a position to nurture potential, one is nourishing or feeding someone who is capable of becoming something; one sees in that person the power to become what has not yet been accomplished.

Mr. Lincoln saw potential in Eugene. He looked through the lens of hope, the lens of possibility. He looked past the negative attitude and the mean spirit of intolerance and saw a young man who had the potential to turn the baggage of his life into something that would enrich the lives of others. By investing in the life of this one student, Mr. Lincoln ultimately enriched the lives of many, many students.

Seeing potential in students and making an investment in their success is a special gift for educators. It might be the most gratifying aspect of spending a lifetime in the classroom, the schoolhouse. As teachers, we leave our fingerprints all over the hearts and lives of our students. Our greatest challenge is to reach that unreachable child. It is the challenge that all teachers must keep before them: to seek out the child who is the most difficult to reach, find the potential that is buried beneath the surface, and invest deeply in that child's future—these are the students who get inside our hearts, under our skin, the students we remember.

Beyond the thought of investing in students, the story of Mr. Lincoln and Eugene provides a rich challenge for the school leader who has opportunities to nurture potential in all members of the school community and in the school itself. What are the lessons to be learned from Mr. Lincoln and Eugene?

Lesson 1: The Hidden Treasure of Potential— Daring to Look Deep

"I'm going to tell Mr. Lincoln," she announced.

"Go ahead, you little brat. I ain't afraid of that n—." Then he stopped. Mr. Lincoln was standing right there.

Now Eugene was in Mr. Lincoln's thoughts more than ever—he knew he had to find a way to reach him.

It is easy to see potential in the teachers and students who perform well, who demonstrate a positive attitude, and who contribute to the life of the school. The trick is daring to look beneath the surface to see the possibility in those who present themselves as least likely to succeed. Mr. Lincoln could have easily looked at Eugene through the lens of hopelessness and written him off as lost—poor performance, negative attitude of intolerance, disruptive behavior, a family that does not work cooperatively with the school . . . why bother with this kid? But Mr. Lincoln got a brief glimpse of what might be, and he made a decision—he would find a way to reach Eugene.

A Principal Reflects

As principals, we receive many letters from parents. Over the years, I saved letters and notes that were especially meaningful to me. This one may be the letter that encouraged me the most.

Dear Principal,

When we had all but given up hope that Emily would be happy in a "traditional" school setting, you said, "Give me a chance with Emily. I'm not ready to give up just yet." Words cannot thank you for the time, patience, and love you have shown to our daughter. You have turned her world around this year from that of a child who cried every day coming to school to a young girl that jumps up in the morning and can't wait to get to school. You are an amazing educator and woman, and we will forever be grateful to you. When you look around and ask yourself, "Have I made a difference?" . . . just look at Emily and you'll have your answer. You have made a difference to us.

Sincerely,
Emily's Mom

Time . . . patience . . . love . . . the ingredients of nurturing potential.

School leaders have opportunities to recognize and nurture potential in teachers and parents as well as students. Teachers are eager for the feedback that will make them realize their full potential. As with students, it is tempting for the principal to gravitate toward the teachers who are performing well, who contribute significantly to the life of the school, who are self-motivated to grow and learn. The committed leader establishes a goal of nurturing each teacher toward his or her full potential. The teacher who is struggling to stay enthused about teaching, who is on the brink of burnout, who is discouraged—this is the teacher who needs to be nurtured. The teacher who has so much to offer but has never heard the encouraging words that will prompt her or him to take the risk, take the next step, go for the graduate degree, take a risk by implementing a new program—this is the teacher who needs to be nurtured.

Teachers need to hear what they are doing well. They should be encouraged to take risks that enable them to grow from good to great. Teachers respond well to being invited to serve on a committee or represent the school at a district meeting. Veteran teachers respond well to being asked to mentor a new teacher or host a colleague for peer observation. Teachers are affirmed when we take the time to say:

- "I need some help working through the master academic schedule this year, and I think you could learn the process easily. Do you want to work with me on it?"
- "I respect how you handle your mainstreamed students. Would you be willing to have one of the other fifth-grade teachers come in and observe you during a lesson?"
- "Your planning is outstanding, especially your assessment strategies. Would you share your strategies with our new teachers who need some help with this?"

Most principals can look back on a time that they were teaching and recall that person in their professional life who came to them and said, "You are doing a great job in the classroom, but I think you have potential to be doing something more. I think you should think about school leadership. Our profession needs people like you to lead our schools into the next decade." Most of us can remember that person, that moment, that word of encouragement. Pass it along!

Are school leaders in a position to nurture the potential in parents? Certainly. Parents, teachers, and principals all want the same thing—a school where their students can learn and grow and flourish, a place that is safe and conducive to learning, an environment that promotes lifelong learning. We all have the same agenda. Parents need to get the message that they are part of the team, that they can make a valuable contribution to the life of the school.

Compared to parents who are not involved, parents who are involved have more positive attitudes and thoughts about the school, and so do their children. However, parental involvement must go beyond cupcake sales and the school carnival. Parents can and should be invited to participate in the education of their children by sharing their expertise with the school, volunteering in the classrooms, helping students edit their writing, listening to emerging readers read aloud, reviewing science fair projects, and sharing their careers with students. The possibilities to move from involvement to engagement are endless. And the best way to get the most difficult, most complaining parent on your side is to invite her or him to come and help out. Recruit that parent for your team, not for the opposing team!

A Principal Reflects

It was one of those mornings when I should have turned around and walked right out the door and started the day over. Before school I needed to go upstairs and meet with the fourth-grade team about upcoming state tests. I arrived back in the office just as the first bell was ringing to discover two critical pieces of information: The teacher on yard duty who supervises students outside before school was absent today, and my secretary was absent today—no subs for either one. Students were running wild in the yard, and the phone was ringing off the hook in the office. It was chaotic.

As I headed to the yard to try to get some control out there, an angry parent approached me, screaming, "This is a mess. Don't you know what you're doing here? I have been trying to call the school for the last 15 minutes—no answer—and then I arrived to find the kids out of control. What kind of a school do you run here?" Of course, my first reaction was to get defensive and tell her that she could not talk to me that way. But I needed help so badly that I heard myself saying, "You know, we really need some help here this morning. Instead of yelling at me, why don't you sit down at that desk and start answering the phone while I go out to the yard and get the kids in order."

The parent did sit down and begin taking phone messages. She stayed for 2 hours, took over 60 messages, and has been an office volunteer every Friday morning since.

Lesson 2: The Patient Gardener— Cultivate and Pull Out the Weeds

"Trouble in the lunch line," Mrs. Belding trumpeted. "He singled out two of our students from Mexico—he called them brown-skinned toads and other unacceptable names."

"I'll take care of this," Mr. Lincoln said quietly. . . .

Just when Mr. Lincoln thought he was making progress with Eugene, there is a major setback. The intolerance in the home where the boy is living spills over into school and has potential to hurt the very person who most wants to help Eugene. "Eugene, my skin is brown, too. This I know, Eugene—someone who loves birds the way you do couldn't possibly have that kind of hate in his heart."

There it is! The nurturer sends a clear message: "I expect more of you than that!"

- To the student who has given up caring about one's work: "You and I both know that you are capable of better work. I expect more of you than that."
- To the teacher who is complaining about a difficult student in class this year: "You would not have that child in your class if you weren't capable of handling the situation. I expect more of you than that."
- To the parent serving as Parent–Teacher Association president who cannot get the members to work collaboratively on committees: "Leaders need to bring out the best in people. I know you can do that."

- To the principal who looks into the mirror and asks, "Are you doing all you can for that child? I expect more of you than that."

When a gardener plants a seed, he or she cannot expect the crop to grow in a day. The seed needs to be nurtured and fed. If the conditions are not just right, some special effort may be needed for growth to take place. There will be weeds and drought, and one day someone may step on the tiny plant, but the patient, loving gardener will continue the nurturing process. The plant will grow. So it is with school leaders when they are striving to nurture potential: Patience, loving patience, prevails in the end.

In our story about Mr. Lincoln and Eugene, the opportunity presented itself for Eugene to hear important words of encouragement:

Then one day Miss Chu burst into Mr. Lincoln's office. "There are two mallards nesting in the atrium!" Eugene and Mr. Lincoln looked at the five perfect eggs in the nest. "Just one problem. The ducklings will need to be near water. They'll need to get to the pond outside. They can't fly like their parents. You'll think of something, Eugene. I know you will," Mr. Lincoln said. And he put his hand on Eugene's shoulder.

Eugene thirsted for and treasured the encouragement given to him by Mr. Lincoln: "I know you will think of something." Think of the students you know who may never hear those words of encouragement and affirmation at home. Think of the teachers who work day after day in the isolation of their classrooms and are never given a genuine pat on the back. Think of that single parent who is working two jobs to keep the family together who desperately needs someone to say, "You are doing a good job with your child."

Students often come to us with experiences that have sent them the message that they are not capable, not likeable, not valued. They have come to expect that they will be regarded as being incapable, unlikable, and not valued. The principal with insight and a willingness to take time with these children will see past that defensive front. He will send a message, loud and clear: "I expect more of you because here every student is valued and important."

A Principal Reflects

Matt moved to our school when he was in the middle of third grade. I could sense from the day that I met him that he had a bit of a chip on his shoulder. His parents were subtle in mentioning that Matt had experienced some behavior problems in his previous school, but they clearly sent me the message that they did not want to elaborate on the matter. On Matt's second day in our school, the lunch aide brought him into the office from the cafeteria. She reported that he had poured chocolate milk over the lunch of the girl who was sitting next to him and then spit on it. When the lunch aide asked him why he had done such a thing, he replied, "That is none of your business."

I was deliberate in making Matt wait to speak to me. He sat in the outside office watching the flow of traffic. I wanted him to feel the positive tone of our school, wanted him to observe the pleasant interactions between teachers, students, and parents that occur in the office this time of day. I wanted him to try to envision himself interacting in a positive way, not in the way that he had learned in a previous situation.

When I met with Matt, I began by telling him that what he did in the cafeteria was not acceptable, that this behavior would not be tolerated at our school. "Did you do things like that in your old school?" I asked him. "Yes," he said. "I am a bad kid. I do bad things all the time." I was ready to accept the challenge. I leaned forward and looked Matt right in the eye. "You may have acted like that in the past, Matt, but we don't do those things in this school. This is a great school. People here respect each other. They treat each other the way they would want to be treated. You won't be acting that way here. I know you can be one of our best students. I expect that of you."

A strange, puzzled look came over Matt's face, as if no one had ever spoken to him that way before. "Okay," he said. "Can I go back to class now?" In the weeks that followed I made it my business to keep a close eye on Matt. I tried to greet him each morning when he got off the bus to get a read of his affect. I checked in with him at lunch and observed him on the playground. He seemed to be getting the message that this was a new place, with new expectations. In the process of nurturing Matt, there were some weeds that grew in his garden, but in the end he had a good year at our school.

Lesson 3: Nurturing the Nurturers—From One to Many

"I'll make you proud of me, Mr. Lincoln. I promise." Eugene Esterhause
was true to his promise. He became a fourth grade teacher.

Mr. Lincoln saw the potential in Eugene to do important things. Eugene did not let him down. He became a teacher and "played forward"
the gift that Mr. Lincoln gave to him when he believed in him. Consider the critical role that school leaders play in nurturing the nurturers, in taking care of the people who affect the lives of students every
day. Teaching can be a lonely profession. The wise principal considers
the power of the learning community. The wise principal assures each
teacher that she or he is part of the community that is growing and
learning together.

The story is told of a man in Ireland who sustained a terrible loss in
his life. Both his wife and his son were killed in an accident. The man's
reaction was to withdraw from the community. He spent day after day,
week after week, in the solitude of his lonely home. Finally, one day, the
local priest came to visit the grieving man. The priest knocked on the
door. The man reluctantly invited him to come in and sit down. Before
sitting down, the priest took the tongs that hung by the fireplace. He re-
moved from the fire one hot coal, setting it on the stone floor in front of
the fire, away from the other burning coals.

The priest stayed in the home of the grieving man all afternoon. He
sat with him in the dark room but did not utter a single word. At the
end of the afternoon, the priest picked up the lone coal that had rested
alone on the cold stone floor. The coal was now cold also, no heat, no
warmth. He held the coal in his hand, and, without saying a word, he
placed it back into the fire. And then he left. As he left, the grieving
man clung to the priest and said, "I will be back. I have been alone long
enough!"

Teachers must be encouraged to draw strength and sustenance from
their colleagues, personally and professionally. The wise principal strives
to make the schoolhouse a place where teachers want to be. The wise
principal models the joy of spending days in a rich and exciting learning
environment. The wise principal models caring, respect, and concern
for others.

A Final Lesson: Planting Seeds of Hope:
Everyone Has Potential

> Mr. Lincoln was the coolest principal in the whole world, or so his students thought. . . . Absolutely everybody thought so except Eugene Esterhause. "Mean Gene" is what everybody called him.

It is critical for school leaders to look through the lens of hope, to see the potential in everyone, to establish and maintain a culture within the school that sends each individual the important message "You are an important and capable member of our school community."

A Principal Reflects: The Scholarship

February 19, 2002. I arrived in Sacramento, California, and as I stepped off the airplane onto the tarmac, I knew that she was gone. Perhaps it was the gray sky, but it seemed more a feeling that swelled up inside me just as my foot touched the ground. Her soul had left this place. A phone call to my sister confirmed that our mom had died 3 hours earlier, while my plane home was still in the air.

After the funeral, I returned to work at the school where I served as principal. I began to think of the $10,000 that I received from my mom after she sold her modest home. I had left it in a bank in Sacramento, in case she needed anything. Strokes and arthritis had ravaged her mind and body in her final years. Mom never needed the money. The bank account had grown to over $12,000. My mom had raised four daughters on a teacher's salary and never had anything near that amount of money. To what use should I put her money?

I felt like she answered the question for me. At my school, eighth-grade graduation was approaching, and 67 of my students would go on to high school. As I headed for bed one night, very tired, the numbers clicked in my head—with interest for 4 more years, that is about $200 per student by the time they graduate high school. Maybe Mom would give each student a scholarship.

My plan began to take shape. I found gold-embossed stationery for the letter that each student would receive in the diploma—a letter to me in which they would tell me what high school they had graduated from, their plans for the future, and where I should send the scholarship check. The letter was folded inside an envelope addressed to me at my home. Yes, this scholarship would be earned by completing high school in 4 years.

No one at school knew of my plan. I simply told the eighth-grade teachers that I would like to award a scholarship in memory of my mother and would need a few extra minutes to do so. No one suspected that every student in the graduating class would be included.

As I went up on the stage on graduation day, I hoped that I would be able to get through this without tears. In English, then Spanish, and Bengali, I addressed the audience:

> Good morning. Welcome to our graduation celebration. *Muy buenos dias. Bienvenidos a nuestra celebracion de graduacion. Shuprovath. Ami apneder que shagoto janai.* Thank you. *Gracias. Donabat.*
>
> This is the time when I usually speak with parents and share some last thoughts with the students of the graduating class. But this has not been a usual year for me.
>
> As many of you know, in February, I lost my mother, Ramona Burnham. My mother was a great believer in the power of education and dedicated her life to it. She taught approximately 1,000 students—kindergarteners and first graders in California and all grade levels in a one-room school house in rural Oklahoma. Nothing would please her more than to continue to contribute in some small way to the education of future generations.
>
> Therefore I would like to award a $200 scholarship in my mother's honor and memory. My mother not only believed in education; she also believed that it is up to us, using our God-given gifts, to earn what we receive. This scholarship will be earned upon graduation from high school in June 2006. The recipient of this scholarship receives today this letter, addressed to me. It will be sent to me when the recipient has graduated high school.
>
> In thinking about our School 2 students in the graduating class of 2002, it was impossible to select just one recipient. Therefore the following student will receive this letter today.

I read the name of the first student, Carlos Aguilar. I could almost hear the students thinking, "Carlos Aguilar? Who could be more average than Carlos Aguilar?" "Miguel Aviles." Again, not a student at the top of the class. "Raquel Aviles, Maria Bonilla, Shaquile Brenner . . ." Soon the students, families, and staff began to realize what was happening. Some cheered their child. Some wept.

After reading the list, I continued:

> Parents, this envelope will be placed inside your child's diploma cover. You may keep this letter anywhere you would like, but may I suggest that you keep it inside your child's eighth-grade diploma cover and then, when the high school diploma is earned 4 years from today and you place it with the eighth-grade diploma, the letter will be there waiting to be mailed to me. This scholarship can be used for a university, 4-year college, community college, trade school, or for expenses as the student enters the workforce after graduating high school. The scholarship is earned by completing high school, and nothing would please me more than to have all 67 scholarships redeemed 4 years from today.
>
> Each student leaves the stage today with his or her first scholarship. It is only seed money intended to plant the idea that if you invest effort into your education, many other scholarships will be available to you.

After a few more words to the students, I left the stage relieved that I had been given the strength to get through this with composure. After graduation I received this e-mail message from a staff member:

> Just wanted to let you know once again how happy I am to be part of this school community. The sense of community was so evident during the eighth-grade graduation ceremony on Friday. Your presentation was superb and from the heart; your mother's scholarship offer was outstanding. The parents were so proud. I was moved to tears.

Now, four years later, I feel like I am about to open a time capsule that I sealed that day. And somehow I think that as I send each letter with the scholarship, in a small way, each student will feel the loving, helping hand that I have felt all of my life.[2]

School leaders have many opportunities to recognize, respect, and nurture the potential in their students. The wise principal considers the words of Louis Pasteur: "When I approach a child, he inspires in me two sentiments: tenderness for what he is, and respect for what he may become" (Blaydes, 2003, p. 54).[3]

CONNECTING TO THE LEADERSHIP STANDARDS: A CASE STUDY—SAVING MR. STEVENS

Recruiting and retaining excellent teachers is a challenge for principals, especially in urban schools. It is critical to this process that they recognize the need for good teachers to feel that they are truly making a difference.

Standard 2

A school administrator is an educational leader who promotes the success of all students by advocating, nurturing, and sustaining a school culture and instructional program conducive to student learning and staff professional growth.

Kathy Rodgers is principal of the Downtown Middle School, a school of 650 students in an inner-city setting. This is Dr. Rodgers's second year as principal. She came to Downtown Middle School after being an assistant principal in a high school in a neighboring district. One of Dr. Rodgers's most critical challenges has been to familiarize herself with the 13 nontenured teachers at her new school so that she can make informed recommendations about giving them tenure. She knows for sure that she will recommend nonrenewal for one second-year teacher but believes that all of the others are going to be okay. One teacher about whom she has no concerns is Craig Stevens.

Mr. Stevens came to Downtown Middle School right out of State Teachers' College 3 years ago. He teaches science to eighth-grade students. Mr. Stevens's classroom observation reports, completed by Dr. Rodgers and the previous principal, reveal satisfactory to outstanding marks in all areas of his performance. It appears that Mr. Stevens is well-liked by his students and colleagues. He establishes a positive working relationship with parents. On a volunteer basis, he runs an after-school chess club for seventh and eighth graders and serves on the School Goals Committee.

As Dr. Rodgers reviews the file of Mr. Stevens, she reflects on how fortunate Downtown Middle School is to have a young teacher like him. She has no reservation that a recommendation for tenure is appropriate. She even considers that Mr. Stevens will someday make a fine principal. Dr. Rodgers schedules a conference with him to discuss his annual evaluation and her recommendation for tenure. However, Dr. Rodgers is shocked with the turn that the conference takes.

After congratulating Mr. Stevens on his successful performance and his valuable contribution to the life of the school, Dr. Rodgers informs him that she is recommending that he receive tenure in the district. Much to the principal's surprise, Mr. Stevens shares with her his frustration with his work. He is discouraged with some of his more challenged students. He is considering leaving teaching. Almost at the point of tears, Mr. Stevens shares with his principal that he feels unappreciated, overworked, and unmotivated. He shares that some family problems have complicated his life in recent months. He is not sure that he is strong enough to maintain the pace that he has set for himself.

Dr. Rodgers believes that Mr. Stevens is worth saving. She wants to help him through this time of decision, help him feel better about his choice to teach, and encourage him to consider school leadership.

Outline a plan of action for Dr. Rodgers to retain novice teachers.

- What are her short-term goals for Mr. Stevens?
- What are her long-term goals for retaining effective novice teachers?
- What activities should Dr. Rodgers include in her plan?
- Dr. Rodgers was surprised about how Mr. Stevens was feeling about his work. What might she do in the future to become more aware of the feelings and morale of her teachers?

TYING IT TOGETHER

- Nurturing potential involves getting beneath the surface—digging for the buried treasure of potential.

- When school leaders make a commitment to nurturing the potential in a student or a teacher, they must acknowledge that growth takes time, that there will be setbacks, and that it will require patience to reach the desired goal.
- Nurture the nurturers. When we take care of each person in our learning community, we are investing in a larger, more critical project than just one person. We are investing in many others.
- There is potential in everyone. School leaders must embrace the mind-set that everyone has potential. The student who appears least likely to be successful is the student who most needs to be nurtured. The teacher who is in greatest danger of failing or burning out is the teacher who most needs to be nurtured.

THE TOOLBOX: NBWA—NURTURING BY WALKING AROUND

Principals can nurture teachers, parents, and students as part of their daily routine. Carve out an hour once or twice a week to walk the building looking for the good things that are happening there. Take with you a stack of sticky notes. When you see something that catches your eye, jot a quick note to the person responsible. Make sure that person gets it as soon as possible. Some examples:

- "Tina, your character education bulletin board looks great. I am sure that all of the students who walk past it each day are learning from it."
- "Steve, I heard a wonderful sound coming out of the music room when I walked by this morning. Most of all, I noticed how much the sixth graders were enjoying their time in your room. Good for you!"
- "Sean, you have such good manners! This morning when I passed you in the hallway, you were so polite in saying 'Good Morning' to me. You are setting a good example for the younger students in our school."
- "Mrs. Johnson, I couldn't help but notice the little notes you put in Jimmy's lunchbox every day. He is eager to read them, and they always make him smile!"

Take time to catch teachers, students, and parents doing good things. Send them the clear message that what they are doing is making a difference.

Peer Observation

Peer observation is a great way to nurture potential in a low-key, non-threatening way. The following steps will get a peer observation initiative off the ground, with little effort and a great deal of benefit for all involved:

- Explain the peer observation initiative at a faculty meeting. Be clear that the purpose of peer observation is for teachers to learn from teachers. Emphasize that this is not for the purpose of evaluation, rather for one colleague to learn from another.
- Ask for volunteers, teachers who wish to spend time observing in the classrooms of their colleagues. If your state or district has a required annual professional improvement plan for teachers, offer this as an activity for it.
- Ask for volunteers to host colleagues in their classrooms for observations. Encourage all teachers—such as music, art, and special education teachers—to consider being a peer observation host teacher.
- Meet with peer observers and host teachers to explain the process. Share the peer observation form (see Figure 4.1) and explain how it will be used. Encourage observers to be creative in planning their observations. For example, a teacher who is having a difficult time with a student who is disruptive might be encouraged to observe in a classroom where a teacher has effective behavior management strategies in place. A classroom teacher might find it helpful and interesting to observe her or his class in another setting, perhaps in the library or the art room.
- Assist in setting up appointments to observe as needed. Provide coverage, if needed, so that teachers can be free to observe colleagues.
- Request that one copy of the completed peer observation report be given to the host teacher and that one copy be given to you. Review

these written reports carefully to see what participants are learning from the observation.

- At the end of the year, meet again with peer observers and host teachers. Facilitate a discussion in which they reflect on the experience in terms of their learning from each other.

Most schools that participate in peer observation report that the benefit is as great for the host teachers as it is for the observing teachers. Teachers report being affirmed by colleagues who believe that they can learn something by spending time in another teacher's classroom. Peer

---

Peer Observation Report
Observer's Name: _____   Date: _____
Teacher Observed: _____   Subject: _____

Comment on each of the areas observed during your visit to this classroom:

Learning Environment

Physical Environment
How is the classroom set up?
How is the classroom decorated?

Classroom Climate
What are students doing during the lesson?
What does the level of engagement and participation tell you about the climate in this classroom?
What expectations does the teacher have for his/her students?

The Lesson
What is the objective of the lesson?
What instructional strategies are implemented to address the objective?
In what ways are the students engaged in learning?
How did you know the lesson was successful?

Classroom Management
How is instruction managed in this classroom—small group, whole group, centers, etc.?
What evidence is there that students are held accountable?
How is student conduct managed in this classroom?

What did you learn?
List three specific things you learned as a result of your visit to this classroom.

Figure 4.1.   Peer Observation Report Form

observation is an easy vehicle for professional growth and for nurturing the nurturers.

Reaching Deep

Use this activity at a fall faculty meeting, after teachers have become familiar with their students and know where the challenges will be this year. Share with your faculty two pieces of literature: the book *Mr. Lincoln's Way*, by Patricia Polacco, and the following poem (source unknown):

I saw them tearing a building down,
A gang of men in a dusty town.
With a "yo heave ho" and a lusty yell,
They swung a beam and the side wall fell.
I asked the foreman if these men were as skilled
As the men he'd hire, if he were to build.
He laughed and said, "Oh, no indeed,
Common labor is all I need."
"For those men can wreck in a day or two,
What builders had taken years to do."
I asked myself as I went my way
Which kind of role am I to play?
Am I the builder who builds with care?
Measuring life by the rule and square?
Or am I the wrecker who walks the town,
Content with the role of tearing down?

- Give teachers time to fill out the "Reaching Deep" form (see Figure 4.2). When the form has been filled out, ask each teacher to place it in an envelope, seal it, and hand it to you. Tell the teachers that they will receive the form back in June.
- At the final faculty meeting of the school year, return the unopened envelope to each teacher. Ask teachers to open the envelope and read what they wrote about the student whom they had selected to "reach deep for" during the year.
- Facilitate a discussion/sharing session with teachers in which they reflect on their investment in the student whom they selected, reporting both their successes and their frustrations.

Reaching Deep

Tribute to a teacher:
To a special person in my life.
Thank-you for *reaching deep* into the corners of my being and
seeing a part of me I did not know existed and others never saw.
Thank-you for your faith in my abilities and my future even when I did not believe.
Thank-you for sharing a part of your humanity and for the spark
that glows warmly inside me.
Thank-you.
Your influence is etched on my soul forever.

My Name _____

Date _____

I want to make a special commitment to Reach Deep to _____

These are the special challenges that _____ faces:
  academic challenges_____
  social challenges_____
  family challenges_____
  physical challenges_____

My goal for _____ is _____

I plan to do these things to address this goal:

These are the people who might help me in reaching this goal:

These are the resources I will seek out in reaching this goal:

I will know I have reached this goal when:

Figure 4.2.   Reaching Deep Form.[4]

- If this activity turned out to be successful for your faculty, make this an annual initiative.
- As principal, fill out one form as well, except instead of selecting a student, select one teacher whom you will nurture during the school year. In June evaluate your progress with making a positive difference to this teacher.

NOTES

1. Blaydes, J. *The Educator's Book of Quotes*, p. 2. Copyright 2003 by Corwin Press, Inc. Reprinted by Permission of Corwin Press, Inc. A Sage Publications Company.

2. This is a true story, shared by Lynn Liptak, who recently retired as principal from Public School 2 in Paterson, New Jersey. It is included with her permission.

3. Blaydes, J. *The Educator's Book of Quotes*, p. 54. Copyright 2003 by Corwin Press, Inc. Reprinted by Permission of Corwin Press, Inc. A Sage Publications Company.

4. Blaydes, J. *The Educator's Book of Quotes*, p. 26. Copyright 2003 by Corwin Press, Inc. Reprinted by Permission of Corwin Press, Inc. A Sage Publications Company.

5

A DRESS FOR THE DUCHESS: LEADERS AS RISK TAKERS

There are risks and costs to a program of action. But they are far less than the long-range risks and costs of a comfortable inaction.—John F. Kennedy[1]

LEADERSHIP LINK 5

Strong school leaders are risk takers. They see problems as opportunities for improvement. Leaders who take risks model courage, and in so doing they encourage others to be risk takers as well.

THE STORY

Brave Irene, by William Steig*

Irene's mother had made a beautiful dress for the duchess to wear to the ball. The problem was that Mrs. Bobbin, Irene's mother, was too tired and too sick to deliver the dress to the duchess in time for her to

---

*Excerpts from *Brave Irene*, by William Steig. Copyright 1986 by William Steig. Reprinted by permission of Farrar, Straus, and Giroux, LLC.

wear it to the ball. And so Irene offered to take the dress to the palace herself!

Irene carefully packed the lovely dress in a box, bundled herself up, kissed her tired mother good bye, and began her journey to the palace. The weather was much worse than she had imagined! It was cold and snow swirled around her as she started across the field to the palace.

The farther Irene went the worse the weather got. Branches were ripping away from trees as the wind blew harder and harder. Suddenly the box containing the beautiful dress was ripped from her hands and the dress blew right out of the box! Even without the dress Irene decided she had to press on to the palace and tell the duchess what had happened.

Tears froze on Irene's eye lashes. She fell into a hole and twisted her ankle. She trudged on into the dark, windy, snowy night, not even sure she was going the right way. Irene had no idea how to reach her goal of getting to the palace and then . . . she had the idea! She would use the box as a sled and slide down the hill toward the glittering lights of the palace. As she approached the palace door she noticed that the beautiful dress her mother had made was plastered against a tree just outside the palace door. She managed to get the dress off the tree and back into the box just in time to ring the bell at the palace door.

The dress was safely delivered and just in time for the duchess' gala party. A joyous Irene was honored for her bravery by being invited to the ball where she enjoyed an evening of music and dancing!

LESSONS LEARNED

Fiction and nonfiction literature is filled with stories of people who are willing to take risks, stories of heroes who are brave and courageous, stories of how change becomes a reality because the leader is brave enough to take a risk or confident enough to encourage someone else to be a risk taker. When Moses led the children of Israel as they fled from the oppression of the Egyptian Pharaoh, he took a risk—he led them straight into the Red Sea!

In 1880, Thomas Edison said, "The photograph is of no commercial value." But he was brave enough, courageous enough, and visionary enough to perfect his own invention, an invention that would pave the way for many more sophisticated forms of technology.

Martin Luther King Jr. had a dream, and his willingness to take a risk changed the very fabric of American life.

Courage, risk taking—how about NASA's astronauts, who are so committed to tomorrow that they risk their lives in search for what is yet unknown. Risk takers are ready at any moment to risk what they are for what they might become.

Brave Irene, as well as other characters in children's literature, welcomes the opportunity to take a risk. Irene, like other characters, shows us how positive change results from embracing courage. School leaders can learn a great deal from stories about bravery and courage.

The character traits of courage, bravery, and risk taking are often used to describe heroes, such as firefighters, astronauts, law enforcement officers, and military personnel. After September 11, we considered the bravery and courage of many of the heroes of that tragic event. We considered the courage of the firefighters who entered the World Trade Center in their attempt to rescue victims of the crash. We considered the passengers on the plane flying over Pennsylvania, headed possibly to destroy buildings in our nation's capital. We even considered the guide dog who led his best friend to safety from the 80th floor of the North Tower. More recently, we have seen and heard about the courage and bravery of military personnel serving in Iraq.

So the question is, do principals need to be courageous risk takers to effectively lead their schools? Or is courage reserved for other kinds of heroes?

There are two important reasons why it is critical for school leaders to be risk takers:

- Leaders are a catalyst for change, and that requires taking risks.
- Leaders who model courage inspire others to take risks.

Sometimes risks are considered activities that are unwanted, something that the individual would choose to avoid. Gambling and drug taking are seen as problematic and destructive. Some risks are sensation seeking, thrills and adventure seeking, disinhibition, experience seeking. The men and women who attempt to climb to the summits of mountains know of and are drawn to the very risk of these activities.

On the other hand, risk taking is considered by some as a desirable, even essential quality of effective leaders. Every leader faces challenges and problems that must be addressed. Problems that present the need to take risks are considered opportunities. Risky situations may be laden with the potential to change what is into what might be.

The first risk that school leaders take is that of the job.

A First-Year Principal Reflects

"I am scared to death of this job! It is such a huge responsibility to lead this school, to be there for the teachers, to earn the respect of the parents, to ensure that the environment is stimulating and positive, and to see to it that students are learning. It is a huge responsibility to ensure the safety of students and staff. At first I asked myself if I had enough courage to do this important work. But I think that that is exactly what draws me to it— the challenge of knowing that it will not be easy, that each day will bring new challenges. Yes, it's a risk, but the work is important."

Indeed, school leaders must be risk takers. School leadership is not for the faint of heart; it is not for those who are afraid to make a mistake. School leadership is not for the individual who is satisfied with the status quo. For school leaders who dig into their work, who sink their teeth into curriculum and supervision, who take on the challenge of bringing each teacher to his or her full potential, who care enough to make sure that the learning environment is safe and secure, every day is a risk, and everyone watches to see how brave and how courageous the leader is. Everyone watches to see if the leader is a risk taker.

In the words of John W. Gardner,

> What leaders have to remember is that somewhere under the somnolent surface is the creature that builds civilizations, the dreamer of dreams, the risk taker. And remembering that, the leader must reach down to the springs that never dry up, the ever-fresh springs of the human spirit.[2]

What can school leaders learn from little Irene, who was determined to give up the safety and warmth of her mother's home and venture out into the storm to deliver the dress to the duchess in time for the ball?

Lesson I: Risks—Problems or Opportunities?

"It's the most beautiful dress in the whole world!" said her daughter, Irene. "The duchess will love it."

"It *is* nice," her mother admitted. "But, Dumpling, it's for tonight's ball, and I don't have the strength to bring it. I feel sick."

Irene and her mother have a problem. The dress must be delivered, and Irene's mother is too ill to do it. Principals face problems every day—small problems and large problems, short-term problems and long-range problems. In most cases, tackling the problem and making a decision to facilitate change requires taking risks. Leaders face a range of problems that can become opportunities for change and improvement.

Personnel Issues

- A principal struggles with the decision about renewing the contract of a second-year teacher who is not performing to expectation.
- A teacher comes to the principal in confidence to report that a colleague may have a drinking problem. The problem is beginning to have a major impact on student learning and the environment in this teacher's classroom. The teacher in question is a member of the community and is married to a local family physician.

Facilities Issues

- A principal searches for classroom space for an additional section of fifth grade so that the district standard of class size can be maintained.
- Teachers in one wing of the building have filed a written complaint that the mold that is growing on stained ceiling tiles is causing them to feel ill and have allergic reactions.

Budget Issues

- There is no money in the technology account, yet the district curriculum calls for students to learn an array of computer skills. In addition, parents have high standards and expectations for the technology program at the school.
- In October, a district-level budget shortfall resulted in a 20% reduction in the middle school budget. The principal must recommend which accounts should sustain the cuts and must explain the rationale to the superintendent.

Student Performance Issues

- Student performance on high-stakes testing fails to meet state and district expectations.
- A new principal discovers that in the previous year, 23% of students in the school were referred for Child Study Team evaluations, a number that is well above state and district guidelines.

Safety Issues

- District resources do not provide the level of playground supervision that the elementary principal believes is necessary to ensure the safety of each student.
- Parents in an urban neighborhood are concerned that the high school does not have a daytime security system. School visitors can enter the building and move about without being checked. The district's position is that it is each school's responsibility to maintain a safe school, but no funds are provided for this purpose.

The need to take risks most often arises from a problem. Although many would say that risks represent unwanted involvement in activities, others see risks as opportunities. School leaders who are risk takers look through the lens of opportunity as they consider how to meet each challenge and address each problem.

There is no shortage of challenges for principals. As principals take on these challenges, they know that they must be risk takers.

Lesson 2: Heading in the Right Direction— Keep Your Eyes on the Prize

> She pushed her lip out and hurried on. This was an important errand. . . . For a short second, Irene wondered if she shouldn't heed the wind's warning. But no! The gown had to get to the duchess! . . . "I can get it there!" said Irene.

Before principals decide to take the plunge, to take the risk to solve the problem, they must have the end in mind. They must know what it is that they need to accomplish. Then they can explore the alternatives that will lead to the desired outcome or goal.

Let's examine some long-range goals that will allow the principal to change the problem into an opportunity (see Table 5.1).

When principals face a problem, they must define clearly and specifically what their goal is. They need to decide what it is they want to accomplish for their school that will make it a better place for students, teachers, and parents. Then they can begin to gather the resources that will be needed to undertake the problem and move forward.

Lesson 3: Lace Up the Boots—Get Ready for the Hike

With great care, Irene took the splendid gown down from the dummy and packed it in a big box with plenty of tissue paper. . . . Irene put on fleece-lined boots, her red hat and muffler, her heavy coat, and her mittens. She . . . slipped out with the big box, shutting the door firmly behind her.

Irene knew that she would be out in the cold as she plowed through the snow to the palace. She would need to dress for the weather and equip herself for the journey. And when she was ready, she stepped out, out into the snow, out into the wind, out to the palace of the duchess. Likewise, the school leader must know what will be needed for the journey and must consider what the conditions will be along the way. And after preparing oneself, the leader must take the step and move forward.

Let's put one of our problems under the microscope and determine what the principal must do to be properly equipped for the challenge.

Personnel Issue.   Marge Johnson is in her second year as a fourth-grade teacher. Her principal, Ken Smith, has been principal at the school for 9 years and was impressed with Ms. Johnson when he interviewed her. He had checked her references, and her work history included 3 years in a neighboring district. During Ms. Johnson's first year, things had gone quite well. She had a class of 18 students and seemed able to handle them satisfactorily. At first Mr. Smith received a few complaints from parents about the fact that she never gave homework, but after he spoke to her about this, it seemed that she began giving some homework. On another occasion Mr. Smith received a complaint from a parent that there were some errors in correcting a math test. Three items had been marked wrong when they were actually correct. Mr.

Table 5.1. A Principal's Problems and Long-Range Goals

Problem	Long-Range Goal
Personnel	
A well-liked second-year teacher is not performing to expectation. The principal must decide whether to recommend nonrenewal of her contract.	Ensure that the quality of teaching and the high expectations that have been established are maintained. Ensure that the climate of the building and morale of the staff are not compromised in the process.
Personnel	
A teacher reports to the principal in confidence that he believes that one of his colleagues has a drinking problem and that the problem is beginning to have a major impact on student learning and the environment in the classroom.	Provide assistance for the teacher with the problem. Ensure that the quality of teaching and learning in that classroom is not compromised.
Facilities	
Class size in the fifth grade is well above district guidelines; however, no additional classroom space is available.	Ensure that all students have the advantage of the class size prescribed by Board of Education guidelines.
Facilities	
Teachers in one wing of the building have filed a written complaint that the mold that is growing on stained ceiling tiles is causing them to feel ill and have allergic reactions.	Provide a physical environment for teachers and students that is safe, healthful, and free of distraction
Budget	
There is no money in the district budget for computers, yet the curriculum requires that students learn an array of computer skills.	Comply with the school's or district's technology plan.

Budget In October, a district-level budget shortfall resulted in a 20% reduction in the middle school budget. The principal must recommend which accounts should sustain the cuts, and explain the rationale to the superintendent.	Ensure that the instructional program will not be negatively affected as a result of the budget cuts.
Student Performance Student performance on state testing fails to meet state and district expectations.	Align the curriculum to district and state standards. Implement high-quality instruction.
Student Performance A new principal discovers that, in the previous year, 23% of students in the school were referred for Child Study Team evaluation, a number that is well above the state and district guidelines.	Refine the referral process so that teachers explore alternative ways to assist students who are academically challenged.
Safety Parents in an urban neighborhood are very concerned that the high school does not have a daytime security system. School visitors can enter the building and move about without being checked. The district's position is that it is each school's responsibility to maintain a safe school environment, but no funds are provided to ensure this.	Ensure a safe and secure environment that is conducive to learning.
Safety District resources have been cut, and the elementary principal believes that there are not enough recess paraprofessionals to adequately supervise the playground and ensure the safety of each student.	Ensure a safe and secure environment at all times.

Smith was puzzled about why the parents were coming to him with these concerns and not approaching the teacher directly. Observation reports had been satisfactory and included, as appropriate, suggestions for fine-tuning various instructional practices. During the summer, a red flag went up when Mr. Smith spent time reviewing and analyzing test data from the state test and noted that the scores in Ms. Johnson's class were, across the board, 15% lower that those of the other fourth-grade classes.

Mr. Smith became more concerned in the second year. Three special education students were mainstreamed into Ms. Johnson's class for literacy and math. Two of these students had behavior issues. Ms. Johnson was unable to handle the students and teach the curriculum effectively. It was necessary for an instructional assistant to go with the students each day from the self-contained special education class to Ms. Johnson's classroom. As the year progressed, Mr. Smith's concerns about Ms. Johnson's effectiveness increased. Often, as he was walking through the hallways, he heard Ms. Johnson yelling at a student. When he would stop into the classroom unannounced, she seemed to be frazzled. There was the sense that the climate was less than positive. Students began to complain to their parents that Ms. Johnson screamed at them. Parents complained to Mr. Smith. During classroom observations, Mr. Smith noticed that the work seemed too easy for the students. Ms. Johnson presented the material at a basic level. She never asked substantive, thought-provoking questions. She seemed to give students a great deal of easy seatwork.

As Mr. Smith reflects on the situation with Ms. Johnson, he knows that he will need to set some goals for her third year, a critical year that will determine if she will receive tenure in the district. As he considers this, he is reminded that Ms. Johnson is well liked by her colleagues. She is active in the Sunshine Committee and helps out with the annual walkathon for childhood diabetes. Last summer she hosted the annual staff picnic at her home on the lake. She lives locally, and her two sons attend the district high school. Mr. Smith knows that dismissing her will not be well received by some of her colleagues. However, when he reflects on her teaching, her classroom management, her interactions with students, and her relationship with parents, he knows that he could do better. He knows that he does not want to bring a marginal teacher onto his team. He decides that he will move forward to build a case for dismissal unless she improves significantly. At the same time, Mr. Smith knows that there is clearly a risk involved. It may compromise his relationship with the faculty and staff, who have come to enjoy Ms. Johnson's friendship and generosity at school. The union will undoubtedly become involved, and the process will get risky.

There is another risk here, of course, and that is the risk involved in not taking action against a marginal teacher. What will parents think if Mr. Smith gives tenure to a person who does not meet the expectations of the school community? What message does it send to the other teachers if a marginal teacher gets tenure? Mediocrity is okay.

Weighing the risks on both sides of the issue, Mr. Smith acknowledges that the easy way out would be to ignore the problem and hope that things improve. However, he knows that he must proceed with a plan that will result in Ms. Johnson's improved performance or her dismissal before tenure is granted. How should he prepare himself for this challenge?

Effective leaders confront problems. They know that problems do not go away by ignoring them. Mr. Smith's plan for Ms. Johnson's third year is to

- identify the professional skills that he expects will be improved,
- define and describe these skills (expectations),
- develop specific activities for Ms. Johnson's improvement, and
- evaluate Ms. Johnson's progress to determine her employment status (see Table 5.2).

With this detailed plan in place for Ms. Johnson's third year, Mr. Smith will be in a position to monitor her progress and make a decision about her tenure contract.

Lesson 4: What Am I Doing Here? Overcoming Discouragement

The wind decided to put on a show. It ripped branches from trees and flung them about, swept up and scattered the fallen snow, got in front of Irene to keep her from moving ahead. Irene turned around and pressed on backwards. . . . Tears froze on her lashes.

Table 5.2. Ms. Johnson's Improvement Plan

Skill Needing Improvement	Specific Expectations	Activities	Assessment
Classroom Management	It is expected that you will manage student behavior in the classroom without yelling at the students. This will require the implementation of a behavior management system that has • Clear expectations for student behavior • Clear consequences for failing to meet expectations • Class incentives for appropriate behavior • Individual behavior plan for the most challenging students	Participate in a full-day workshop on classroom management (during the summer). Engage in peer observation of well-managed classrooms. Consult with Child Study Team for assistance with mainstreamed students.	Formal and informal classroom observations by principal and district supervisor

Communication With Parents	It is expected that you will establish and maintain effective communication with parents throughout the school year.	At Back-to-School Night, present a well-defined plan to parents outlining your classroom procedures, your homework policy, and highlights of the curriculum. Publish a periodic newsletter to parents that outlines curriculum highlights and class events. Respond to notes and calls in a timely manner.	Provide copies of the periodic parent newsletter to the principal.
Curriculum	It is expected that you will follow the approved curriculum and differentiate instruction to meet the needs and abilities of all students.	Participate in a mentor relationship with a veteran fourth-grade teacher who knows the curriculum well and whose students perform well on state tests. Plan with your mentor; observe her teach and how she differentiates instruction.	Maintain a log of meetings/interactions with the mentor. Include reflections on what you have observed and what you have learned. Meet periodically with the principal to review and discuss your reflective log.

The storm intensified, and things got worse for Irene. In moving forward to address the problem, the school leader needs to know that things will probably get worse before they get better. Along the way to a successful outcome, the road will be bumpy, and there will surely be difficult times. Let's consider principal Janice Stewart, who is struggling with what she should do about Marcia Jones, a fifth-grade teacher who is suspected of having a drinking problem.

Janice is a first-year principal at an intermediate school in an upper-middle class suburban community. The principal who proceeded her had been at the school for 29 years, was well loved, and lived in the community. He knew two and three generations of families. He had hired all of the staff, which Mrs. Stewart inherited. One of Janice's first priorities was to get to know her new staff. She was making an effort in the first semester to make informal classroom visits and meet with teachers to get to know them and to build relationships.

Janice had to admit that she was not surprised when Bill Jacobson, one of 6 fifth-grade teachers in the school, came in after school one day to tell her about his concern for one of his colleagues, Marcia Jones. Mr. Jacobson reported that the entire fifth-grade team knows that Ms. Jones has a problem with alcohol. They have reason to believe that she drinks during the school day, when she goes home for lunch. They are critically concerned that things are not going well in her classroom. Students are off task a great deal of the time, and many behavior issues are interfering with student learning. Based on informal visits to Ms. Jones's classroom, Janice had already noted concerns about the climate in her classroom and about Ms. Jones's pattern of poor attendance and tardiness.

As Janice considers the situation, she knows that this will not be an easy one. Ms. Jones is a local resident, and her husband is a medical doctor in the community. She is well connected socially to many people in town, including some Board of Education members. She and her husband are personal friends with the previous principal and his wife. Janice knows that confronting this situation as a first-year principal will not be easy. Indeed, in addressing a highly sensitive problem such as this, things will probably get messy and complex.

It is critical that school leaders be deliberate in their effort to anticipate the complications that arise as they proceed to address a sensitive problem. Before approaching the problem, do an informal risk assessment:

- What messy, complex challenges are likely to arise along the way?
- Are these challenges ones that I can manage, or will it be necessary for me to bring in additional resources?
- What support should I line up before I begin to confront the problem?
- Do I know of other school leaders who have confronted a similar problem? Can I call on those colleagues for advice and guidance in approaching the problem?
- What will it take for me to reach a successful outcome?

Anticipating the challenges and being prepared to address them with confidence and commitment is the key to reaching a successful outcome.

Lesson 5: Creative Solutions—They Said It Couldn't Be Done!

She laid the box down and climbed aboard. But it pressed down in the snow and stuck. She tried again, and this time, instead of climbing on, she leaped. The box shot forward, like a sled.

It would have been easy for Irene to say, "This just can't be done!" It would also be easy for the principal to say, "There just isn't money in the budget to do that, so I guess it can't be done!" But principals who have determination and are willing to take a risk say, "We have to figure out a way to make this happen, with or without budget support."

Principal Rosemary Rogers has a problem that requires creativity. The district technology budget has sustained drastic cuts. There are no funds to purchase new computers. Teachers are eager to teach computer skills and use technology to enhance their classroom teaching, refine their communication with parents, and create teaching tools. What is frustrating is that there is no reliable technology in the building. Not every classroom has a computer. About half of the classrooms have at least one good computer. The lab, which is located in the media center, has only 10 computers. The equipment is not new. At any given time, it is unlikely that more than 8 of the computers are up and running. During a computer class it is necessary for two or three students to share each computer. Teachers who wish to communicate with parents or their colleagues via e-mail are frustrated. Most of them do not have working computers in their classrooms, and the few computers in the media center are in constant use by students.

Rosemary knows that she must find a way to bring technology into the school—with or without district funds. She reminds herself that the plan will require some creative, out-of-the-box ideas. She sits down to sketch out the following plan:

- Create a technology committee made up of teachers and parents, including representatives from the Parent–Teacher Association.
- Formulate a vision for the implementation of a technology initiative; develop rationale.
- Make arrangements for committee members to visit other schools to learn about their technology programs. Learn about curriculum, teacher and staff training, hardware and software needed, and space required in the building.
- Determine the technology hardware and software that will be needed to achieve the vision.
- Investigate funding possibilities, including grants, corporate sponsorship, and fund-raising.
- Present the committee's proposal, which includes budget needs to teachers and parents; attempt to get buy-in from all groups.
- Kick off a technology initiative campaign to raise funds for the plan. Write grants; seek corporate matching funds, possibly through parent workplace connections; and ask the Parent–Teacher Organization to dedicate fund-raising to the initiative.

Leaders must be committed to a vision and a successful outcome. Eliminate from your vocabulary, "Yeah, but . . ." There is no room for the "Yeah, but . . ." mind-set if leaders want to change obstacles into opportunities.

Lesson 6: Time for a Party—Celebrate Success!

What a wonderful ball it was! The duchess in her new gown was like a bright star in the sky. Irene in her ordinary dress was radiant. She was swept up into dances by handsome aristocrats. . . . Her mother would enjoy hearing all about it.

Irene celebrated the successful delivery of the duchess's dress by attending the gala ball. School leaders often forget the value and importance of celebration. One year after the initial meeting of Rosemary Rogers's School Technology Committee, the school had a 25-computer lab fully functioning in the media center. This was made possible by a grant from a major Internet provider, collaboration with a local university, and a successful fund-raiser organized by the Parent–Teacher Organization. To celebrate this impressive accomplishment, the school hosted an open house and a ribbon-cutting ceremony. Parents and teachers visited the new lab. The principal publicly acknowledged and thanked the committee members and sponsors who made the vision a reality.

A Final Lesson: Strong, Confident Leaders Encourage Others to Take Risks

> "Come to the edge of the cliff," he said.
> "We're afraid," they said.
> "Come to the edge of the cliff," he said.
> "We're afraid," they said.
> "Come to the edge of the cliff," he said.
> "We're afraid," he said.
> They came.
> He pushed.
> They flew.—Author unknown

It is critical for school leaders to take risks. Solving problems involves taking risks; facilitating change involves taking risks; moving a school forward into uncharted territory involves taking risks. However, there is yet another reason for school leaders to take risks. Leaders who demonstrate courage and model risk taking encourage others to take risks.

Teachers need to be encouraged to try new instructional strategies, to be lifelong learners, to stretch themselves to do something that they have not tried before.

A Teacher Reflects

At first I thought she was kidding. My principal asked me to consider *looping* with my class next year. I had read a little about looping, and I understood that it involved having the teacher and the class move together to the next grade. For me it would involve taking my first graders to second grade. I had taught second grade several years ago but recently had gotten comfortable in first grade. Our school had never tried looping. It would be something new, and I was not even sure how parents would like it.

However, my principal had a vision, and she wanted me to be part of it. Looking back on it now, my first year of looping was the best thing that I could have done for myself professionally. There is so much about this model that is good for kids. In the end the parents loved it. Now we do it every year—I rotate between first and second grade every other year. I think what meant the most to me was that my principal respected me enough to involve me in something that was new and risky. The night that we met with the parents to talk to them about it, she said, "I would only ask an outstanding teacher to engage in looping." Her public affirmation meant a great deal, and it made me willing to take the risk.

Risk and Encouragement: The Principal on the High Ropes Course. I had been a principal for 6 years when I received a grant to be used for professional growth and development activities. I chose to use the grant to participate in Harvard University's Summer Institute for School Leaders. Spending 2 weeks on the Harvard campus was an amazing opportunity, and I met many impressive school leaders from around the world.

A highlight of our time at the institute came on the Saturday between the 2 weeks that we were in class. We were required to rise early on Saturday morning and board a small boat, which took us out into the Boston Harbor to Thompson Island. We spent the day actively engaged in outdoor-adventure team-building activities. Honestly, on that hot, sticky morning no one was too happy about this activity.

As luck would have it, my group was assigned to the high ropes course. Our group of 12 principals trekked through the woods to the site where this activity would take place. The task was explained to us: We would climb up a tree about 12 feet. Then we would walk from that tree to another one by edging along a rope that was stretched between the two trees—a span of about 25 feet. To steady yourself you could hold onto a rope that was stretched parallel to the rope where your feet would be.

When you arrived at the second tree, you would climb up again, about another 10 feet, and cross over to the final tree by walking along another rope. This time, however, there was no parallel rope. Instead, you could hold onto a series of three ropes that hung vertically from above. Reaching the third tree was the goal.

I sat on the ground and listened intently as the task was explained. I heard our instructor say, "You don't have to try this if you don't want to, but you should know that each one of you is capable of completing this high ropes course." I decided to watch and see how others made out with the challenge.

The first one to try the course was a young, fit, athletic-looking man who was a principal in Colorado. He shimmied up that first tree, crossed the first rope, climbed the second tree, and spanned the rope to the last tree with little effort. He was lowered down, and the whole group celebrated with him. The next person to try it had a little more difficulty. After faltering a number of times, he did complete the course. The third person gave up and came down when he got to the second tree. A few decided not to try it at all.

From the ground, I watched each person try the task. I watched where they put their hands, where they put their feet, how they leaned their body into the ropes, where they fixed their gaze. And I started to talk to myself, "This is your chance. You will never know if you can do it if you don't try!" And so I jumped up and said, "I'll go next!"

I had no problem climbing the first tree, and even the first rope span was not too bad. I had watched carefully and knew that it would work out best if I leaned forward into the upper rope. I was okay climbing the second tree also until I realized something about the ropes that were hanging vertically. My arm span was not wide enough to reach between the ropes—I would have to let go of one rope before I could grab the next one. I paused to think this through and try to make a decision about whether I should go on.

That's when I heard them—my colleagues sitting on the ground looking up at me: "You can do it!" "Go for it!" "You are doing great—keep going!" Their encouragement was just what I needed to take the risk. I did go for it, and I completed the course. When I was lowered down my encouragers gathered around me in celebration.

That day I learned a great deal about taking risks and receiving encouragement. I had many opportunities in the years that followed to play forward that sense of encouragement to others. There are many teachers, parents, and students in schools who need someone to cheer them on. They will take the risk if someone tells them they can do it.

CONNECTING TO THE LEADERSHIP STANDARDS: A CASE STUDY—TERRIBLE TEST SCORES AT VILLAGE SCHOOL

This case examines the challenges faced by many principals in the era of high-stakes testing. Test scores in this school fall below state and district expectations. Out of a commitment to promoting the success of all students, the principal knows that he must confront the challenge with a clear plan in mind. He must keep his eye on the goal of increased student performance. Recognizing his responsibility as the school's instructional leader, he realizes that confronting critical issues relevant to the school's culture and instructional program will involve personal and professional risks.

Standard 2

A school administrator is an educational leader who promotes the success of all students by advocating, nurturing, and sustaining a school culture and instructional program conducive to student learning and staff professional growth.

Thomas Jackson has been principal of the Village Intermediate School for 2 years. One of two intermediate schools in the blue-collar community of Westford, the school houses 660 students in grades 4, 5, and 6. Mr. Jackson has worked hard to improve the morale of the staff, a problem that he identified early in his time at Village. The staff is a blend of veteran teachers and new teachers. In the last 2 years, Mr.

Jackson has been able to hire six new teachers. He has five tenured teachers who are burnt out and resistant to any change that comes along.

A major concern of the teaching staff is class size of 28–30 students. Mr. Jackson acknowledges that this is not good for teacher morale. Neither is it an optimal instructional situation for students.

The greatest problem facing Mr. Jackson is the poor performance of his fourth graders on the state tests. In the area of literacy, 54% of the fourth graders passed the test, achieving a status of proficient or advanced proficient. Forty-six percent performed at a partially proficient level. Math scores are even worse. Forty-eight percent passed the test, and 52% scored at the partially proficient level. To add to the challenge, at the other intermediate school in Westford, which has similar demographics, the fourth-grade scores are significantly higher. Only 19% are partially proficient in literacy, and 24% in math. Parents at Village School are beginning to ask the question "Why is our school performing at such an inadequate level?"

Mr. Jackson knows that he must take some drastic measures to address the problem of low test scores. His reading specialist and math specialist, both of whom are well respected and knowledgeable in their curricular areas, believe that the curriculum is a large part of the problem. Many times they have expressed that the curriculum is not relevant to their school's population. Students are not getting the basic skills that will prepare them for success on the state tests. However, the district prides itself in having an ambitious curriculum that raises the bar for students. Mr. Jackson knows that departing from the approved curriculum will be risky.

In addition, Mr. Jackson notes that the team of fourth-grade teachers has some weak links. Two of the fourth-grade teachers who have taught for over 25 years are openly resistant to any change.

As Mr. Jackson considers his challenge, he realizes that making major changes that will bring about an improvement in test scores will involve certain risks. Changes in the curriculum or in how the program is delivered will likely cause problems with teachers and the curriculum office. On the other hand, he knows that students could and should be doing better and that parents are asking for better results.

Mr. Jackson has made the decision to initiate a comprehensive plan to improve test scores. Outline a plan of action that will be a blueprint for Mr. Jackson to use. In designing your plan, consider the following:

- What are the short-term and long-range goals?
- Outline a specific, detailed action plan for improving test scores.
- What are some of the potential risks for Mr. Jackson if he moves forward with a plan for change? What are the risks if does not?

TYING IT TOGETHER

School leadership is risky business. Personnel issues, safety matters, facilities concerns, budget constraints, and issues relevant to student performance—these are the kinds of problems that require the school leader to take action.

- Problems present the need to take risks. Wise leaders see a problem as an opportunity laden with exciting potential that it will improve the life of the school.
- When leaders take risks and begin to confront the problem, they should have a clear goal in mind. They should carefully consider the short-term and long-range outcomes.
- Leaders who take risks must equip themselves for the challenge. A well-defined plan of action—including clear goals, vision, and creativity—is critical to a successful outcome.
- Implementing change that will address a problem involves challenges. Change is not easy.
- Celebrate successful outcomes.
- Strong, confident leaders encourage others. Leaders who are risk takers encourage others to take risks.

THE TOOLBOX: ACTIVITIES TO ENCOURAGE RISK TAKING

School leaders are encouraged to use the chart in Table 5.3 to plan and organize a response to a problem.

Table 5.3. Problem-Solving Action Plan

Problem: *State the problem. Why is it a problem?*

Primary Goal: *What is the main goal that you want to accomplish as a result of the action plan?*
Secondary Goals: *What other positive outcomes might occur as a result of the action plan?*
Risk Assessment: *What risks should you be aware of before confronting the problem?*

Activities *What activities will you initiate to achieve your goals?*	Timeline *When should this activity be initiated? Completed?*	Person Responsible *Who will be accountable for the completion of this activity?*	Resources Needed *What resources (funds, materials, time, personnel, support) will be needed to accomplish this activity?*	Evidence of Completion *What evidence will indicate that this activity was successfully completed?*

NOTES

1. Blaydes, J. *The Educator's Book of Quotes*, p. 205. Copyright 2003 by Corwin Press, Inc. Reprinted by Permission of Corwin Press, Inc. A Sage Publications Company.

2. Retrieved February 20, 2006, from http://leadershipnow.com/risktaking quotes.html.

6

STAY IN THE CITY:
CHANGE OR TRANSITION?

Change is an inevitable journey. All things are constantly changing, transforming, becoming something different. Guiding change so that it is successful is what leadership is all about.—California School Leadership Academy[1]

LEADERSHIP LINK 6

School leaders focus on the need for change more than the change itself. They understand how to take the journey from what is to what can be. Leaders know that the transition is more important than the destination.

Now the Little House only saw the sun at noon, and didn't see the moon or stars at night. . . . She didn't like living in the city. At night, she used to dream of the country and the field of daisies and the apple trees dancing in the moonlight.°

°Excerpts from *The Little House*, by Virginia Lee Burton. Copyright 1942 by Virginia Lee Demetrios, renewed 1969 by George Demetrios. Reprinted by permission of Houghton Mifflin Company. All rights reserved.

THE STORY

The Little House, by Virginia Lee Burton

Once upon a long time ago there was a beautiful Little House in the country. She was built on the hill and could see the countryside all around her. In the evening, Little House could see the lights of a big city in the distance. She wondered how different it would be to live there. As time went on, the horses and carriages gave way to the horseless carriages, trolleys, and trains. Blacktop roads replaced the dirt pathways. Soon apartment houses, stores, and schools began to appear all around Little House. Steam shovels began to dig. Tall skyscrapers soon replaced the apartment houses. Little House was sad and wanted to go back in time so she could once again look out and see the city in the distance. One day, a young woman happened to discover Little House almost squashed in between the skyscrapers. "Why, this was the very house that my grandmother lived in many years ago!" she shouted. But it is not in the country any longer. The young woman decided to move Little House back to the countryside. She fixed her up to look new and beautiful again. Little House was happy in her new location. It was quiet and peaceful in the country.

LESSONS LEARNED

What is it all about? Why, change, of course! School leaders believe that they must initiate and sustain change in schools. The challenge is that most people want to hold on to what they have. The longer the change has been around, the more difficult it is for them to give it up. People naturally resist change. Even the Little House longed to go back to the way things were. It is a natural tendency in all of us to want to hold on to the familiar and not let go. But change, like a ripple that originates from a rock thrown into the pond, can slowly drift out and permeate an entire school. It continues to spread until it encompasses the entire pond. In between the ripples, the water remains calm.

There is a rhythm in the ripples. Likewise, there must be a rhythm or cycle as things change. In between the ripples, the wise leader creates calm. There must be time to refresh, to rest. And the turbulence caused by each ripple must be just right.

Leaders encounter resistance whenever changes are introduced.[2] The Little House resisted the change of the emerging city environment and eventually went back to the country. Principals who understand change as process, who know that they should focus on the journey and not the destination, may wind up staying in the city and accepting the change rather than going back to the country. Let's take that journey together to understand how leaders should approach change.

Lesson 1: Leaders Must Tell the Story— Why Do We Need Change?

> The Little House was very sad and lonely. . . . So they jacked up the Little House [and] . . . slowly moved her out of the city.

Little House was not convinced that there was a need for a city to sprout up around her. She wanted to go back to the way things were. She liked the serene countryside. She did not see a need to change.

People are like the Little House. Why should they change if they do not see a need for change? When they understand the need for the change, then and only then do they accept the change.

Leaders do not focus on the change. Instead, they focus on the need for change. Leaders must first convince others that there is something that needs to be changed. Unless followers agree that something must be corrected, improved, or replaced, they will continue to resist the changes that are proposed.[3]

People may be drifting away from the school's vision. Student outcomes in reading or science may have to improve. Teachers may be asked to differentiate instruction to accommodate diverse populations. Maybe it is time to revisit the school's mission, change the organizational structure, or initiate a new curriculum process. All of these changes cause turbulence, but the more that followers understand the need for change, the less turbulent it will be.

Each of us perceives the need for a change differently. For that reason, the leader must spend time telling the story. Why is the change needed? What will the journey be like as we leave the familiar and move on to the new? If the leader convinces others that there is a need to change, followers will begin to walk along the leader's path. The wise leader gets followers to understand the need for change. Then change can begin to happen!

Lesson 2: The Change Plan—Making the Quilt

> They went along and along, but they couldn't seem to find just the right place.

The Little House had no plan. She started out by saying that she wanted to go somewhere but was not sure exactly where. In the famous Anderson fairy tale *Alice in Wonderland,* the Cheshire cat asks Alice where she would like to go. Alice replies that it really does not matter much. The cat quickly responds to Alice that if she just keeps on walking, she is bound to get somewhere (Carroll, 2000).

If you set out on a journey and just keep traveling, you too may wind up somewhere but perhaps not in the right place. Leaders understand change as process more than change as product. They understand that how one gets to the change is just as important as the change itself. Leaders develop a plan for change. Take the journey step by step with me.

First, picture the change.[4] As you begin to plan, let your imagination lead the way. You must reshape your ideas. Begin to think outside the coffee cup. Learn a lesson from Starbucks. If Starbucks continued to create coffee flavors and drinks, perhaps people would visit their cafes less frequently. Instead, Starbucks has been transforming coffee cafes into cyber cafes around the country (Hamel, 2002). Think different. Let the familiar begin to give way to the new. Do not get stuck on what is. Look for what might be.

Second, become passionate about the change. Passion is powerful.[5] If you reach deeply inside of yourself and you do not feel passionate about the change, why should anyone else be excited about it? The passionate leader inspires change. Our passion ignites the spark in others and gives a sense of purpose to the change. Imagine what the change looks like, feels like, smells like, sounds like, and tastes like. As you begin to dip your brush into the pallet to paint a picture of the change, use bright creative colors that attract followers.

Third, believe that it is possible. Listen to your inner voice and know that the change you are proposing is realistic.

Fourth, transform rather than tinker. Leaders know that change begins with what we value and believe. They know the difference between technical and adaptive changes.[6] Adaptive changes focus on values and beliefs, which are integral to the school's culture. Technical changes focus on management and structures. Adaptive changes are substantive. Technical changes tinker around the edges. When we begin to plan for change, we must consider the school's culture, its core values. What do we really believe? What do we value?

If we want to revisit grouping, for example, adaptive change will focus on reaffirming our commitment to a culture that values equity. We can then look at the technical changes that may be needed to achieve that goal. How will we group students—homogeneously or heterogeneously? Schools too often examine the technical aspects of a change. They may never get at the adaptive change. We may never talk about equity for all students within the context of the grouping process.

Fifth, limit changes. Think of all the changes going on right now in your school. Pause and make a list. How long is your list? Do you have 5 changes, 10, more? At a workshop about change, I recall asking an audience this question. One person had a list of 20 changes going on in her school.

Sixth, create connections. Are the changes connected in some meaningful way to each other, or are they disconnected?

Now you are ready to develop a change plan. The staff will accept a coherent plan more easily than they will individual, isolated, or disconnected changes. As you implement the plan piece by piece, each patch enhances the beauty of the new quilt.

Lesson 3: Change—A Five-Step Dance

Everyone seemed to be very busy and everyone seemed to be in a hurry.

Just as the Little House perceived the hustle and bustle of the big city, leaders often believe that they must move along, change quickly, have lots to do, meet deadlines. I recall my participation with a Fulbright group in Italy. We arrived, unpacked, and took a walk together. As we strolled down the streets of Rome, I asked one of the directors about my flight home. As we turned the corner, my eye caught the Colosseum. The director and I stopped to look at this marvelous ancient structure. She said, "The Colosseum was here, is here, and will be here for a long time. Why are you asking about your flight home? You just arrived. Take your time, enjoy the moment."

Change, too, takes time. Let's learn the five-step dance together.

Step 1. Change is a process. It evolves. Begin with a plan. Develop a timeline. There are no quick fixes. As we lead others through adaptive changes, the technical, organizational, and managerial changes will take time.

Step 2. Change requires a culture in which accountability is valued. Everyone must be accountable for success. If the reading scores are not acceptable in a middle school, the reading or language arts teachers should not think that they alone are accountable for success. Every teacher must be accountable. Every teacher should begin to implement skills that improve literacy outcomes. The social studies, science, and math teachers have to become accountable to improve the reading scores, not just the reading teachers. Everyone is accountable for success.

Step 3. Change works best in schools when everyone shares in leadership roles and responsibilities. In a school where the principal knows when to lead and when to step out of the way and let followers become leaders, a culture of collaboration begins to emerge. Resistance to change is minimized. Continuous improvement and lasting change is valued. Leaders should not expect that mandated, top-down changes will be embraced by followers.

Step 4. Change happens in teams. Recall the difference between groups and teams. Change is more successful when teachers work collaboratively rather than individually. Leaders must know how to create highly effective teams.

Step 5. When leaders build trusting relationships with followers, change becomes acceptable. These relationships result in a synergy that bonds the community of leaders and learners. Recall the spider spinning its web. The more threads that it creates, the stronger the web. So it is with people. The stronger the relationships, the more they become willing to change.[7]

Lesson 4: Potholes, Sandboxes, and Kites

The air was filled with dust and smoke, and the noise was so loud that it shook the Little House.

When you tell someone to change, you are really telling her that what she has been doing is no longer valued. Change can be insulting, especially to experienced teachers. Imagine an art teacher using the same projects each year with third graders. The principal comes along and tells him that he must introduce new projects with his students. Throw out the familiar. Change!

The teacher becomes anxious and may even fear the change. This approach affects the trusting relationship between the principal and the teacher. Potholes begin to appear in the road. Change becomes difficult for both of them.

When we approach change this way, the art teacher, in this example, may begin to think about his own competency. "Does my principal think that I am not an effective teacher? Besides, what expertise does she bring to this discipline? After all, I am the art teacher and who knows best but me?"

It could be quite difficult to get an experienced art teacher to integrate new projects into his teaching. The longer he has been in the position, the more reluctant he may be to change. Perhaps the principal is the only one who is excited about this idea. More potholes in the road.

If the staff becomes skeptical or resentful of the changes that are going on, the leader must rely on her influencing and supportive behaviors. She must spend time with teachers. The principal must focus on the individual. Teachers must relearn, revise, realign, and reimagine, or more potholes will appear in the road.

The odds are against you that people will embrace change. Imagine a roomful of people who have just settled in to listen to you speak. Before you begin, ask them to stand and change their seats. Eyeball the room. Watch the body language and turbulence emerge. Once everyone is seated, pose the question, "When I asked you to change your seats, what was the first thing that came into your mind?" The answers are revealing. You may hear, "Who are you to ask me to change my seat?" or "Hey, I want to sit next to my friend and now I can't." These are the responses that I hear each time I do this.

Now, just imagine what it will be like when you ask the staff to change the math program. How about asking your staff to reorganize from a self-contained middle school to one in which teams work with groups of students for 2 years. If people resist changing their seats, all the more reason for them to resist changes in organizational structures or programs. Resistance is a natural phenomenon.

Ninety percent of heart-bypass patients cannot change their lifestyles, even if they risk dying (Deutschman, 2005). If that is true, changing people's non-life-threatening behaviors is going to be tough. Watch out for the potholes.

How can leaders avoid some of the potholes? First, tell stories about the change that you need. Second, model the behaviors that you are trying to change. If you want people to take risks, try new ideas, then leaders must also take risks, be willing to try new ideas, and create a culture in which risk taking is safe.[8] Third, invite others to come into your sandbox and play with you. Lessons from the sandbox facilitate change (Gregerman, 2000). Play; be enthusiastic; and explore with a sense of wonder, curiosity, creativity, and innovation. Sponsor discussion groups around breakfast or lunch. Initiate book clubs. Encourage your staff to plan a few recreational trips together during the holidays or in the summer. Go to a play, a museum; plan a hike or bike ride on a brisk fall morning. Celebrate with your staff. Present the Golden Plunger Award for the change that did not turn out as expected.

The wise leader knows that change is like flying a kite. The leader knows when to let out more string, when to hold steady, and when to pull back. Leaders know how to work around the winds of resistance.

Lesson 5: Change Is the Wrong Concept—
It's All About Transitions

A cellar was dug on top of the hill and slowly they moved the house from the road to the hill.

The movers gave all the support needed to the Little House as it traveled from the city to its new location in the country. During this transition, the Little House was happy once again.

Transition is the journey away from the familiar and toward the new.[9] Leaders let followers take something familiar with them as they travel toward the new. When children go to a pajama party, they are excited and anxious all at once. They want to go to their friend's house, the new place. They like sleepovers. They have a fun time. Yet, they are anxious. They do not want to let go of the familiar—their home and its comfortable surroundings. How do they solve this dilemma? Children bring something familiar with them as they travel to their friend's house. They choose their favorite teddy bear, toy, or something else to hold onto. Maybe it is their blanket or a pillow. As they prepare to leave home, Mom or Dad is supportive and encourages the risk. The children arrive clutching the familiar while embracing the new. They are making the transition.

Adults are no different. Giving up something familiar is difficult for them. They begin to complain, blame, get upset, and even become angry. They want to go back to the familiar. Leaders have to understand this process. If they focus on the transition and give their support to those who are asked to take the journey from the familiar to the new, then the change becomes more acceptable to everyone.

A Principal Speaks

An experienced principal had a conversation with the staff: "We are going to make a transition from our current reading program to the new one. I am here to support you along the way. If you want to bring along some of the strategies and materials that we used with the previous reading program, that's alright. I know it's not easy to make transitions. As we take this journey together, I am hoping that you enjoy the new program." This principal understands how to hold on to the familiar and make a transition to the new.

The principal continues, "There will be some potholes along the way. We will fill them in as we travel along the road. We will make it work. We will arrive at our new destination together."

Principals must paint the picture. They must tell the story about the need for the change. Principals must be passionate about the change, believe that it is possible to achieve and that it will make a difference for the students.

A Final Lesson: What Is It All About?

Change is all about transitions. Leaders must focus on the need for making the transition, and they must support followers as they begin their journey. It is all about understanding change as process. The Little House did not understand the need for change. She wanted everything to remain the same. Unlike the Little House, who was moved from the city back to the country, leaders may have to keep people in the city. If that is going to happen, leaders must understand the importance of speaking the language of transitions. Leaders who focus on the individual and build trusting relationships can make a difference with change. Make the transition together, and most people will follow, but do not forget to bring some teddy bears along!

CONNECTING TO THE LEADERSHIP STANDARDS: MENDING MORALE

Ms. Califon, principal of an elementary school, is experiencing staff morale problems as a result of the recent hiring of a new assistant principal.

Standard 3

A school administrator is an educational leader who promotes the success of all students by ensuring management of the organization, operations, and resources for a safe, efficient, and effective learning environment.

The principal of a suburban K–6 elementary school, Ms. Califon, hired Mr. Alteri, the new assistant principal. The former vice principal, Mr. Lee, left the school to accept a position as principal in another district. He was well respected by a majority of the staff. Before being appointed elementary school assistant principal, Mr. Lee worked in the district for 15 years as a science teacher in the middle school. He had a strong presence as vice principal in the elementary school. The staff, students, and community admired and respected him. Teacher morale was strong during his 5 years as assistant principal. People characterized the climate in this elementary school as being open. The leadership team was supportive, and the staff was collegial.

In September, Mr. Alteri arrived. Soon he began to initiate some changes. His ideas were met with resistance. The turbulence increased when he began to tinker with the schoolwide discipline code and the lunch and hall duty schedules. Mr. Alteri believed that these changes were going to improve the climate of the school. After all, he wanted the school to have a safe, efficient, and effective learning environment.

During his first 3 months as vice principal, a number of issues surfaced that created moderate turbulence with the staff. A sixth-grade special education student, Jeff, was the elected representative to the student council. According to the bylaws of the student council, a student can be dismissed from his representative position because of inappropriate behaviors that occur inside and outside the classroom. This includes a student's behavior in the lunchroom or on the way to and from school.

Jeff was frequently misbehaving in the lunchroom and on the bus, and he always offered excuses to Mr. Alteri. Much to the disappointment of the teachers, the assistant principal allowed Jeff to continue to be a student council representative. The teachers suspected that Jeff was manipulating the situation. He knew how to play the game.

In January, Mr. Alteri started to plan for the sixth-grade 2-day trip to Gettysburg, Pennsylvania. He was excited about leading this special event. However, the teachers were apprehensive. They believed that Mr. Alteri was too easy, a pushover with student discipline. They also believed that he was a poor manager. The lunch and hall duty schedules had to be changed four times before he got it right.

Ms. Califon decided to meet with the teachers who were going to Pennsylvania. She asked that they make this a successful event for Mr. Alteri despite the fact that they did not want him to be in charge of it. The teachers requested that Ms. Califon come instead. Ms. Califon declined their request.

It was difficult to build trusting relationships with Mr. Alteri. He began to observe teachers and write evaluations that were more critical than supportive. When he did not see evidence of cooperative learning groups or the use of technology during his observation, he made comments about the teacher's not meeting the needs of all learners in her or his classroom.

As time went on, teachers continued complaining about Mr. Alteri. They finally filed a grievance against him for violating contractually defined observation procedures. The principal knows that she needs to get involved before the situation deteriorates further.

- How can the principal accurately assess the level of turbulence that exists in the school because of Mr. Alteri's actions? What should she do about it?
- When Ms. Califon received the initial complaints about Mr. Alteri, how should she have responded to the teachers and to Mr. Alteri?
- How should Mr. Alteri respond to the grievance? What should Ms. Califon's role be in the grievance process?
- If Mr. Alteri felt a need to make some changes in the school, what could he have done differently?

TYING IT TOGETHER

- Leaders focus on the need for change. Leaders tell stories to convince others that the change is needed.
- Picture the change. Become passionate about the change. Believe that it is possible. Make a plan. Change is a process.
- Leaders nurture a culture of accountability that allows everyone to take responsibility for the change.
- Watch out for strong winds. Know when to let out more string, when to hold steady, and when to pull back. It's like flying a kite.
- Change is all about making a successful transition. Make sure that everyone has an opportunity to bring along their teddy bear as they transition from the familiar to the new.
- Change takes time.

THE TOOLBOX: CHANGE AS TRANSITION

Sit down with the staff members and ask them to complete a chart similar to the one shown in Table 6.1. List all the transitions that are underway at your school.

Table 6.1.   Transitions Assessment Chart

What's changing?	What is the level of turbulence created as a result of this transition?			What is the level of resistance that others have toward this transition?			What is the staff's level of competency in implementing this transition?			How essential is this transition within the context of our school's vision and mission statement?		
	Mild	Moderate	Severe	Mild	Moderate	Severe	Limited	Moderate	Adequate	Not Essential	Important	Essential

Here are some prompts to guide the staff through this process:

- *What's changing?* This is a list of all the transitions that are currently underway at the school level or district level. Once each participant completes the list, it should be refined through consensus building. This results in a list that everyone can accept.
- *What is the level of turbulence created as a result of this transition?* Gross (1998) indicated three levels of turbulence in school organizations. Mild turbulence is normal and usually causes no disruptions in the work environment. Moderate turbulence is caused by widespread transitions. They have an effect on most members of the organization. Conversations in the workplace focus regularly on the transitions that are underway. Stress becomes obvious throughout the organization. Severe turbulence gets everyone's attention. Stress is high. The values and beliefs that make up part of the school's culture are at risk. Severe turbulence can cause disruptions and significant anxiety.
- *What is the level of resistance that others have toward this transition?* Mild resistance indicates that a small group of staff (less than 10%) is actively resisting the transition. Moderate resistance indicates that a larger group of staff (10%–50%) is actively resisting the transition. The resistance is growing stronger. Severe resistance indicates that half or more of the staff is actively resisting the transition. The resistance is growing stronger every day.
- *What is the staff's level of competency in implementing this transition?* Limited competency indicates little or no professional development before or during the early stages of implementation. Moderate competency indicates that there was some professional development before the implementation began, and at least two or more opportunities will be provided for professional development during the transition process. Adequate competency indicates that some professional development was provided before the implementation began. There will be regularly scheduled opportunities for professional development throughout the transition.
- *How essential is this transition within the context of your school's vision and mission statement?* If the transition is perceived as not essential to your school's vision and mission, the participants should

We should defer these transitions (changes) for another time:	We should continue to discuss these transitions (changes) before proceeding:
We must provide additional professional development before continuing with these transitions (changes):	We should develop a plan for these transitions (changes):

Figure 6.1.   Assigning Priority to Transitions

evaluate this transition as not essential. If the transition is important but not essential, this transition should be evaluated as important. If the transition is important and essential to the school's vision and mission statement, the transition should be evaluated as essential.

Once the staff arrives at a consensus, ask the members to place each of the transitions in the appropriate box (see Figure 6.1).

This process assists the staff and principal in identifying the essential transitions that should become part of a coherent schoolwide plan. Connect each of the essential transitions to the school's vision and its mission statement. Finally, connect each transition to develop a coherent plan for change.

NOTES

1. Blaydes, J. *The Educator's Book of Quotes*, p. 72. Copyright 2003 by Corwin Press, Inc. Reprinted by Permission of Corwin Press, Inc. A Sage Publications Company.

2. Bob Evans (1996) discussed the key sources of resistance to change. He approached all school improvement and change through the lens of process more than product.

3. The need for change—and the importance in planning for change—is discussed in Duke (2004).

4. People need to see a picture. Making the idea become real through pictures is discussed in chapter 5 of Bridges's *Managing Transitions: Making the Most of Change* (2003).

5. In *The Passion Plan*, Richard Chang (2000) discussed a systematic approach to discovering, developing, and living your passion.

6. In *Leadership Without Easy Answers*, Ronald A. Heifetz (1994) explained the differences between technical and adaptive changes.

7. In *Implementing Change: Patterns, Principles, and Potholes*, Hall and Hord (2001) discussed the 12 principles of change, including change as process, leadership styles, and the importance of teams.

8. In *Changing Minds: The Art and Science of Changing Our Own and Other People's Minds*, Howard Gardner (2004) wrote about the importance of storytelling and embodying the story that we tell in our own lives.

9. On the importance of managing transitions, see Bridges (2003).

7

THE STORM: LEADING IN A CRISIS

Leadership is being visible when things are going awry and invisible when they are working well.—Tom Peters[1]

LEADERSHIP LINK 7

School leaders have the capacity to lead with calm strength. During a crisis in the life of a school, the leader must model courage and attend to the needs of others. They know to look for the joy that can arise from pain, and they know to share it with others.

THE STORY

Tornado, by Betsy Byars*

When a tornado appears on the horizon, farmhand Pete gathers the family into the storm cellar. It is a frightening time for the family, especially because Daddy is out in the field as the tornado approaches. He

---

*The story and the quotes in this chapter are from *Tornado*, by Betsy Byars. Copyright 1996 by Betsy Byars. Used by permission of HarperCollins Children's Books, a Division of HarperCollins Publishers, 1350 Avenue of the Americas, New York. All rights reserved.

cannot make it to the house in time to get into a safe place with the family! Pete has endured many tornados in his lifetime. He knows that it will help the family if he can keep their minds off of what is going on outside.

Pete tells the children the story of Tornado, a black lab who arrived at his childhood farm during a tornado. Tornado got his name because his doghouse had been lifted into the air and dropped into Pete's yard! Pete immediately fell in love with the gentle dog.

As the storm raged above the storm cellar, the children listened intently as Pete shared his memories of Tornado—how the dog learned to play a card trick, how he almost ate the family's pet turtle, and how he dug a large hole in the dirt to keep himself cool on hot summer days.

The children were absolutely on the edge of their seats as Pete told them about the day he and his father took Tornado to town with them and another family claimed the dog as their own. They said his real name was Buddy! And so Tornado was returned to his rightful family, but not for long. He found his way back to Pete and stayed there from then on!

A happy ending to Pete's story and a happy ending to the tornado— Daddy returned safely from the field as soon as the storm passed. Stories of Tornado, the very special black lab, had helped the family get through the storm without being afraid! Pete's wisdom, experience, and storytelling turned a scary day into a day the children would long remember!

LESSONS LEARNED

What is the role of the school leader during a crisis in the life of a school? In the recent past, many books and articles have been written on crisis management. This is not one of those. Rather, this chapter examines the role of the leader during a crisis and the leadership qualities that provide strength and calm during troubled times. In an effort to distinguish between managing a crisis and leading in a crisis, the chapter examines how a strong leader models courage and calm; cares for others during the crisis; and seeks to see the beauty, the opportunity, that can grow out of a crisis. Any manager can learn to manage a crisis; it is the true leader who can recognize the needs of the people affected by the crisis. A true leader models strength and calm and in the wake of the crisis tries to see the beauty that grows from pain.

A crisis is a situation of great difficulty or danger, a difficult or stressful event, a condition or period of insecurity. A crisis involves a decisive or important turning point. Interestingly, the Chinese symbol for crisis is a combination of two other symbols: danger and opportunity. Danger and opportunity—powerful concepts that leaders must understand.

The story *Tornado* has many lessons that can help school leaders consider the unique challenge of leading a school through crisis.

Lesson 1: Houston, We Have a Problem!

"Twister!" he shouted again. My mother was standing outside the door. She was worried about my daddy. . . .

"He's in the cornfield," Pete said. "He can't hear you, m'am." . . . "He'll be all right. He can get in a ditch. You come on now."

She ducked into the cellar, and Pete pulled the door shut behind her.

Pete knew that this was a crisis. He knew that this was not just a rainy day or an evening thunderstorm. This was a tornado, and Pete knew that a tornado would put the family in danger. He knew that things could get worse before they got better. Pete knew that he had to act quickly and deliberately, even when he met resistance from Mother, who was worried about her husband, out in the field. Pete knew that he had to assume a role of calm, strength, and courageous leadership if the family were to survive this crisis.

Many challenging situations come before the school leader on a daily basis. Some require an immediate response from the principal; some can be handled by the principal's designee; and some will take care of themselves. Some situations are serious and require immediate attention, but they are not crises. To respond in an appropriate manner, prepared principals need to identify if, in fact, the situation that confronts them is a crisis. Prepared principals know that a crisis is a situation that

- affects the entire school community,
- may get worse before it gets better,
- may require outside resources to resolve it,

- may get out of control, and
- is susceptible to rumors and hysteria.[2]

If a high school student has been injured in a car accident over the weekend, it might not be a crisis; however, if the accident occurred after a party during which at least 50 high school students were drinking and using drugs, the school may need to respond in crisis mode. If a teacher breaks up a fight in the school cafeteria between 3 eighth-grade students, it might be seen as routine discipline. If the students were members of a gang, the school may need to respond in crisis mode.

Using farmhand Pete from our story *Tornado*, the school leader must first be decisive and take quick and deliberate action.

A Principal Reflects[3]

It was only the second spring that our young middle school faced, and our efforts to batten down the computer system had become porous. Smart, capable students had found ways to infiltrate the administrative network, to the point where teacher observations and evaluations had been found open on student terminals in a computer lab. But a break finally came. We discovered a student-created website containing our school's administrative passwords, which allowed us to trace the hacking to two individuals. The first, Jeremy, was sent home with his father on a 10-day suspension at about noon on the first Friday in May. He was dispatched to his home after a stern warning about his near-criminal behavior and a reprimand to use his creativity and energy for good instead of deviance. The meeting with the second student's parents was taking place in my office after school the same day. My administrative assistant knocked and then peered into the office to inform me that our juvenile officer requested to speak with me immediately on a telephone outside my office. I excused myself from the meeting and took the call at the receptionist's desk in the main office.

"Steve, Jeremy hung himself this afternoon," I heard through the receiver. My mind raced. I tried desperately to make sense of what I had heard. This was surely a figurative message from our officer, who was most likely trying to help counsel our young man toward making better life choices. With a sense of panic, I uttered the only word I could muster, "What?" "Jeremy hung himself at home this afternoon. I am at the house now, and he was unable to be resuscitated. He's gone, Steve."

My world stopped. My mind raced. Impossible. I just spoke with him. I just sent him home. I put down the receiver. With hot tears trying to squeeze out from behind my eyes and with hands cold and trembling, I abruptly ended the now-meaningless meeting taking place in my office. I quickly huddled with my assistant principals and whatever counselors and student assistance faculty were still in the building. We tried to think. None of the training on the principalship, none of the courses on leadership, none of the in-service and practical experiences, none of the manuals on crisis equipped or prepared me for this. Raw humanity infiltrated the science of leadership, leaving in its wake a test of strength and stamina that few experience in professional life.

As if on automatic pilot, we attempted to move forward. Our first hours included responses to logical and mechanical necessities, such as developing a crisis-response plan with the superintendent and district personnel. Then my two assistant principals and I got into a car and headed to Jeremy's home, believing that a visit from us was necessary to personally convey the deep loss felt in our hearts, to make an immediate move beyond fear to show compassion, love, and care. The ride was silent, disquieting. Questions of why and the wondering of blame cycled like runaway locomotives in my head. What words would come when I greeted the parents who only hours before had received news from my lips that their son had engaged in computer hacking? What words would fill the chasm between that news and the tragedy that now befell them? Wanting to turn back but pushing forward under the sage counsel of a compassionate and insightful assistant, I stood with grieving parents in the entryway of their center hall colonial home. Words became irrelevant. Communicating a grief-stricken heart simply required being present and making human contact.

The visit was short but significant. It marked the course that leadership would take as our school community recovered from this tragedy, a course that would not self-preserve or avoid risk of reprisal but one that would show heart and the strength found in valuing relationships.

The response to this crisis ran on parallel tracks. The first dealt with the technical details necessary to care for an entire school community. The second covered my response of needing to lead when wanting to flee. On the technical side, a well-represented crisis team met for much of Saturday to vet and address every contingency that the group could muster. Personally, however, the test of leadership had just begun.

With news of the suicide running rampant through the school community via instant messaging, it quickly became apparent that faculty and students were upset by the loss of their classmate and for what might happen to me as the perceived impetus of the tragedy. On Monday morning, I would be required to face our faculty first and then students to convey a message that would stretch beyond fear to what mattered most, grieving the loss of one of our own. Wanting to hide yet standing before faculty in our early-morning meeting and then broadcasting live via the school's television studio to students, I was unwilling to cover the emotion attached to our loss. I expressed our sorrow, our collective love for Jeremy, and our plans for getting through this first day. It was imperative that the message be one that balanced compassion with confidence, sorrow with hope, and planning with allowing grief to follow its natural course. The message could neither blame nor accept blame. It could not make Jeremy a hero or a villain. It could not demonize those who may be or become angry at me for taking disciplinary action. It must convey heart and life, leadership and strength.

On Mother's Day, 2 weeks later, the headline of the local paper read "Parents Blame Suspension for Student's Death." An emergency faculty meeting was held the next morning. Angry, hurt, and defensive faculty members were quick to suggest that they respond with an editorial or letter to the editor rebutting the article and defending me as the primary target. Once again it was time to lead. On that early Monday morning, encouraged and bolstered by the love of indignant faculty, I once again found the strength to move beyond my own needs to focus on what mattered most. The pain of accusation was nothing compared to the loss of a child. Grieving always involves blame and anger when searching for elusive answers. Regardless of the circumstances, our school would not lose sight of the primary consequence: A family was left childless in the wake of a great tragedy. Our hearts would steadfastly show compassion, not anger, and understanding, not defensiveness. We would look toward healing and wholeness. We will always be about people.

Leading in a crisis requires that one becomes immersed in the perspective of those with the greatest loss. It requires one to set aside personal interest to focus on what is most significant.

As a footnote, many stepped forward to minister to me as I moved through this crisis. Good friends cried with me; colleagues took me golfing to clear my head; family sustained and loved me; and mysterious guests appeared and then disappeared simply to inform me that there was information that few knew regarding the precipice this student had been on for some time. Through it all, I was reminded that school leaders lead people, not schools. And people matter.

Lesson 2: A Day in Paradise? Don't Be So Sure

Along about lunch, it hit . . . there was no warning . . . no funnel cloud, no nothing. One minute we were eating beans and biscuits at the table. The next there was a roar—worse than a train—worse than a hundred trains. And then there came a terrible tearing sound, like the world was being ripped apart. I can still hear it in my mind.

The tornado hit without warning. Pete had planned to work in the cornfield that day; Mom had planned to do some baking; the boys had hoped to go fishing. But the tornado changed all of that.

School principals know the challenge of efficient time management. So many interruptions characterize a day in the life of the principal— a phone call from a concerned parent about the bus driver, a substitute teacher who is unable to handle the class, a report from the custodian that there was vandalism to the back of the school over the weekend, a "quick question" from a teacher that turns into a tearful breakdown about being overwhelmed with the class. These things are not crises; these are the typical interruptions that come before the principal each day.

The organized principal will set up the day to try to make the most of the time: conduct the morning walk-through, set up a meeting with the Parent–Teacher Organization president, keep an appointment for a classroom observation, set aside time to return phone calls, and carve out time to visit the cafeteria and interact with the students. And every now and then the principal actually has a day that is running close to schedule . . . until someone delivers the bad news, until the crisis occurs.

A Principal Reflects: Playing With Three Strings—
Reflections on the First Anniversary of September 11[4]

When world-renowned violinist Itzhak Perlman performs, his preparation process is lengthy and almost painful to watch. Using crutches and braces that support his polio-stricken legs, Perlman slowly walks onto the stage, sits down, places the crutches on the floor, moves his legs into position, and after a final tuning signals the conductor to begin. An apocryphal story is told of a performance in which Perlman went through this lengthy preparation and began to play, only to have one of his violin strings suddenly snap a few minutes into the concert. The stunned audience sat quietly as the music stopped, fully expecting him to make his labored way offstage to replace the string or tune another violin. Instead, they watched as Perlman remained seated with his violin, adjusting and listening to the sounds of the remaining strings. After a few minutes, Perlman again signaled the conductor and proceeded to perform the entire concerto on three strings.

What was the result? That evening, the audience heard beautiful sounds that had never been heard before. The quality of the music, its depth and resonance, was Perlman at his superlative best. Why? Because the master had accepted a challenge and stretched his prodigious talent beyond what he had ever done before. The result was magical.

In many ways, this tale is a reflection of what we have been doing in our schools since September 11. That morning, just as we were tuning our schools for another great year, one of our strings snapped. For a brief moment, the beautiful harmony that characterizes effective schools stopped. We were stunned and frightened, not only for the children in our care, but for our families and friends. On that day and in the days that followed, we knew that our lives and the lives of the children would never be the same.

But the music of education had to resume, and all of us in the school community quickly learned how to make music with just three strings. The string that snapped was the one that played tunes of innocence, joy, and laughter. The music goes on, and in many ways we are playing a melody that has beauty, meaning, and depth previously unknown.

In looking back, we have been able to distill some good things from the horror of September 11. Our students' response to the tragedy has been to gain new perspectives for such desirable qualities as perseverance, compassion, devotion, courage, and kindness as exemplified by those who responded to the crisis.

Just as the virtuoso's string snapped when he least expected it, so did school leaders find themselves plunged into a crisis on what had promised to be a perfect day. There is no choice but to tune the other strings and make music with what you have.

Lesson 3: Hold Hands and Hold On!

> My two brothers ran from the barn. Pete helped my grandmother down the steps. "Hurry up, boys," she called. Then she said to my mother, "Come on, Beth."
>
> My brothers and I sat on the dirt floor. My grandmother sat on a pickle barrel and my mother on an orange crate. We sat for a moment, silent. We listened to the storm.

Pete took charge. He knew the importance of being together during the tornado. Even when Mother hesitated to enter the storm cellar because she was worried about Daddy, Pete knew that she had to be with them. He knew the power of holding hands and holding on.

During a crisis in the life of a school, the leader must focus on the need for people to be together, to support each other in a safe, nonthreatening place where the reality of the crisis is processed. In part, this is a function of communication. Teachers often feel that they work in an isolated, sometimes lonely environment. They go into their classroom, close the door, and shut out the outside world. Opportunities for adult interactions during the day are limited. However, during a crisis, members of the faculty and staff need to be well informed and well connected to their colleagues. The leader needs to provide a setting where teachers can come together to be informed, to grieve, and to support each other.

A Principal Reflects

Rick—our school's beloved, crazy, impossible band director—lost his battle with cancer on a Thursday morning. We all knew it was coming. Rick had stopped by to visit at school about 3 weeks earlier—we knew that his visit would probably be the last time that we would see him. His 16-year-old son Jason called that morning and told us that his dad was gone.

The school day had started, and teachers were in class, but Rick's friends and colleagues deserved to know. I sat down and crafted a short memo to the staff:

> I have very sad news to share with you this morning . . . our friend Rick has lost his battle with cancer. He passed away early this morning after a valiant fight with a relentless disease. I will keep the door open all day if anyone needs to come in and talk, and let's get together just after school in the library to remember Rick and all that he has meant to us and to our school.

I knew that we should spend some time together remembering Rick, and we did . . . and it helped. As soon as dismissal was completed, teachers began to come into the library. I had set up the coffee pot and put out a plate of cookies. Kevin, the vocal music teacher who shared a room with Rick, began by saying what a great guy Rick was: "Did you know that Rick spent extra time with the special education students so that they could be in the concerts like the other kids? He just wouldn't give up on them." Sharon, our school secretary, shared how supportive Rick was after her kidney transplant: "He always asked how I was doing, and he let me know that he really cared by the way he listened to me." Janet recalled Rick's strong faith and how his strong and brave battle with cancer was an inspiration to us all.

Our time together that day remembering our friend Rick helped us get through a tough loss, and it drew us closer together as a school family.

Lesson 4: Walking the Talk—All Eyes on the Leader

We listened to the storm and worried about my father in the cornfield. Something that sounded like gravel was thrown against the cellar doors. "Hail," my mother said, and bowed her head.

Pete cleared his throat. "You know what this brings to my mind?" he said. We knew, and my brothers and I turned to him gratefully. We saw a flash of teeth as he smiled at us . . . Pete settled his straw hat on his head and began. "I remember it was an August day, a whole lot like this one."

In our story, Pete knew that the family was nervous and worried. Father was still out in the field. The wind was howling, throwing stones and dirt against the door of the storm cellar. The situation had all the ingredients for a panic situation. Pete knew that he had to set a tone of calm and strength. The young boy telling the story was grateful when Pete smiled and began to tell the stories that would keep everyone's mind off of the scary situation. Had Pete shown fear or panic, the group would have taken that lead from him. How the leader responds during the crisis clearly sets the tone for the reactions and responses of teachers, students, and parents.

A young school teacher who taught in lower Manhattan recalled how her students responded to the attacks on September 11. She remembered how every eye was on her. She gathered her students to a safe place away from the windows so that they could not look outside at the tragedy. She spoke calmly to them and tried to assure them. But what haunted her in the days and months that followed was her keen awareness that it was not her words that reached her students; it was that every little eye was on her. Students never took their eyes off their teacher, whom they loved and trusted to get them through.

In a school, everyone watches the principal. The strong leader acts with confidence, demonstrates concern for those affected, communicates clearly and efficiently, and finds strength in the midst of distress.

A Principal Reflects

I was a first-year principal when I was confronted with a tragic, heartbreaking situation. One of our active parents failed to come for her usual time to volunteer in the library. Although it was not like this parent to miss her time at school, we did not think too much about it. After all, it was getting close to the holidays, and people were extra busy. Her two sons, in Grades 1 and 3, were dismissed as usual and took the short walk home. What they found when they entered their house would change their lives forever. Their mother had taken her own life by hanging herself in the foyer of their beautiful home. The boys ran outside and down the street, "Someone, help my mother!"

Teachers who knew this family were shocked and hurting. The day after the funeral, a group of teachers told me they wanted to visit the family at their home. Was I planning to go also? We made arrangements to walk over to the house together after school. As we got close to the house, the teachers stopped and asked me to go in first, "Will you go first? You will know what to say." My first thought was that no course that I had taken, no professional book that I had ever read, could have prepared me for what I was being asked to do. What could I possibly say to these two little guys who had just suffered such a traumatic loss? But quickly I knew that the challenge before me was more than reaching out to those little boys. I also needed to help these teachers through this experience. The only way to do this was to lead with kindness, serenity, and compassion.

A Final Lesson: Buried Treasure—The Unexpected Bonus

"Storm's over!" he cried.

We rushed out through the cellar doors and into the fresh air. . . .

My older brother said, "I wish you had told the story about Tornado and the rooster. That's my favorite."

"Next time," Pete promised. Then he winked at me. "If there is one."

Pete had to walk away from the storm cellar that day feeling that his commitment to the family, his strength, and his wonderful stories had made a difference during a difficult time. Leaders who are willing to step forward, take charge, stay calm, and reach out to people may find the unexpected bonus. They may find an incredible opportunity to make a difference. The wise leader looks for these opportunities and draws from them the strength and passion to lead on.

A Principal Reflects

I first met Alexa the summer before she started kindergarten at our school. Her mother had asked if they could meet with me to discuss Alexa's adjustment to kindergarten. When I met Alexa, I understood her mother's concerns. Alexa had lost her hair to chemotherapy.

Alexa made a smooth and uneventful transition to school. By school picture day, in October, her hair had grown in enough for her to have her picture taken without her little hat. She was having a great kindergarten year.

As I walked into the office early on the morning after spring vacation, the phone was ringing. It was Alexa's father. "The doctor has spotted another serious problem . . . very serious. I wanted to let you know that Alexa won't be back in school for the rest of this year." One never knows what words to use when a father shares such horrible news about his little girl, but I heard myself saying, "My husband and I are both very healthy, and we give blood regularly. If Alexa needs blood, we hope you will call us."

The call for blood came in June, but there was a serious complication. Alexa's blood type was rare—AB-negative. My husband is AB-negative, and he sprung at the opportunity to give blood for her. In July, Alexa and her family headed to South Dakota for a pediatric bone marrow transplant. It was not until the first week in August that I heard from them again. I was sitting by the pool reading when the phone rang. It was Alexa's father calling from South Dakota: "She's not doing well at all . . . very sick, very weak. We have told the doctors here about your husband's blood, and they are wondering if he could give for her today." Within an hour we were at University Hospital, where the blood was taken and then air-lifted to Alexa, 2,000 miles away. The call later that evening told me that this 6-year-old girl and my 40-year-old husband had a very special chemical connection: "We wanted you to know that she responded immediately when she received the blood. Thank you!"

Alexa returned home in September and was doing well except for one thing—she was not able to produce her own platelets. Of course, my husband became her platelet donor. Back then, when you gave platelets, you lay flat on your back with both arms strapped down. The blood was taken from one arm, taken up to a point where the platelets were extracted, and then the blood reentered through the other arm. The process took as much as 2 hours. My husband gave platelets for Alexa twice a week for 6 weeks.

One day after giving platelets, he called from the car on his way back to the office: "She's not taking the platelets today. I think something is wrong." I called the hospital and reached Alexa's mother, who was at Alexa's bedside. "What's going on? I hear she's not accepting the platelets today." What I heard brought tears of joy: "She's not taking his platelets today because today is the day that she started making her own platelets!"

Alexa is in college now. She recently sent us a Christmas card with a note to my husband: "Don't forget . . . I want to dance with you at my wedding!"

Sometimes great joy and satisfaction come out of a crisis. Sometimes because we are the principal, we have an incredible opportunity to really make a difference. Watch for those beautiful opportunities, because they will strengthen you when the next challenge arrives.

CONNECTING TO THE LEADERSHIP STANDARDS: A CASE STUDY—DISASTER ON A FIELD TRIP

School principals take on the ever-challenging responsibility of ensuring the safety of teachers, staff, and students. As daunting a task as this is, it becomes an even greater challenge when students are off campus for field trips and curriculum-related excursions. This case study deals with a crisis that occurs on a field trip.

Standard 3

A school administrator is an educational leader who promotes the success of all students by ensuring management of the organization, operations, and resources for a safe, efficient, and effective learning environment.

Mr. Perez is principal of an elementary school in a suburban community 50 miles south of New York City. Today, 84 fourth-grade students from his school are on a field trip to the science museum, which is approximately 40 miles from the school. Four teachers and 12 parents are accompanying students on the trip.

The two school buses leave promptly at 8:30 a.m. At 9:15 the school receives a telephone call from the state police, informing Mr. Perez of the following:

- The lead bus was involved in an accident with a tractor-trailer on the interstate highway.
- There are reports of many injuries, possible deaths.
- Injured students, parents, and teachers have been transported to three nearby hospitals.
- Students on the second bus witnessed the accident.

Develop a plan to respond to this crisis. Consider the management responsibilities and the leadership responsibilities in responding to this situation.

Crisis Management Responsibilities
- What is the role of the principal in this situation?
- Who needs to be notified, and how should this notification take place?
- What is the sequence of events that must be put into place in response to this crisis?
- What is the role of the police in this situation?
- Who will speak to the media?
- What is the role of the crisis management team?

Leadership Considerations
- What tone should the principal create to get the school through this crisis?
- What are the needs of the students? the injured? the witnesses? What role does the principal have in attending to the needs of students? What additional resources might be required?

- What are the needs of the parents on the trip? the parents of the injured? the parents waiting for news of the accident? What role does the principal have in attending to the needs of the parents?
- What are the needs of the teachers on the trip? their colleagues back at school?
- How should the principal communicate with the staff?
- How does the principal's behavior, actions, and attitude influence students, parents, and teachers?

TYING IT TOGETHER

A school crisis requires more than management. It demands strong, confident leadership.

- The leader must determine if the situation at hand is in fact a crisis, and the leader must respond appropriately to keep people safe and calm.
- Preparation is critical. On the day that we least expect it, a school may find itself in the midst of a crisis. Develop a crisis management team that will be poised to handle a crisis when it occurs.
- Caring leaders acknowledge the need for people to be together during a crisis. Provide opportunities for members of the school community to huddle during the storm. During a crisis, hold hands and hold on.
- All eyes are on the leader during a crisis. How the leader conducts herself during the crisis becomes the model for those who are watching.
- Sometimes beauty is waiting to shine through a crisis. A wise leader looks for the beauty and shares it with others. Beauty adds meaning to the pain.

THE TOOLBOX: COMMUNICATING DURING A CRISIS

The communications that follow can serve as models in a crisis that involves the death of a student.

Communicating With Staff

Dear Staff,

This letter delivers some very sad news to our school family. Julie, one of our fifth-grade students, succumbed to cancer this morning at University Medical Center. I know that many of you knew and worked with Julie in recent years and that you share my sadness at the loss of this very special child.

I have been in touch with Julie's family and have expressed to them the condolences of our entire school community. They will let me know as soon as the funeral arrangements have been made. I will then pass this information along to you.

If there is anything I can do for you individually or collectively during this sad time, please know that I am here and that I share your sadness.

Sincerely . . .

Communicating With Families

Dear Families,

It is with great sadness that I inform you of the loss of one of your child's classmates, Julie. As you know, the class has been very concerned about Julie's illness. I have visited the classroom on numerous occasions in recent weeks to attempt to answer their questions about her condition. They have been wonderful in making cards for her and writing letters to keep her up to date about what has been happening in school. This is a loss that each of them will feel very deeply.

Respecting that each family may wish to handle the conversation about death in its own way, we chose not to announce Julie's death to the class this afternoon when we received the news. I know that each of you will handle this discussion in a way that is consistent with your religious and cultural beliefs. We will have counselors here at school beginning tomorrow morning. These professionals will be available to your child if he or she feels the need to speak to someone.

Julie's family has asked that the school's response be to create a walkathon in her memory to raise money for childhood cancer. In the next few weeks we will begin to make plans for this activity. I mention it now because it is often important for young children to feel that they are doing something in response to a loss. You might share with your child at this time that they will have an opportunity to participate in an activity that will help other children like Julie.

Thank you for your ongoing support and encouragement. Be sure to hug your child tonight!

Sincerely . . .

Communicating With the School Community: Julie's Eulogy

I am pleased for this opportunity to share, on behalf of our school community, some memories of a very special little girl named Julie. Julie was a bright, inquisitive student who asked good questions and gave great answers. She was an avid reader and a passionate writer. She participated in our REACH program for gifted and talented students. But what we remember most about Julie is that she was a spunky, feisty little kid who had a mind of her own. And when she set her mind to something, there was no changing it.

Julie's teachers tell me about her desk. It seems that Julie kept a very messy desk. She saved everything and stuffed things into the back of her desk to the point that she couldn't find the things that she needed. When her teacher would ask her to clean out her desk, Julie would find papers stuffed into the desk that had been there since the first day of school! Resistant to throwing anything away, Julie always had a very good, very logical reason why she should save her papers. And there was no changing her mind. We loved that about Julie!

Julie was always so proud and happy when her mother came into the classroom to share with her class about the Jewish holidays. Julie was so proud of her culture and her heritage and was excited to share it with her classmates. We loved that about Julie.

Julie's fourth-grade teacher tells me about a time last year—before we knew of her illness—when one of our teachers was diagnosed with leukemia. Students had been told that this teacher was very sick and would be out of school for some time. Of all of the students in the class, Julie was the one who kept wanting to talk about this teacher. She asked about him often and was anxious to hear how he was doing. It is ironic that it was this same teacher who was with Julie and her family on Friday afternoon, when the end came for Julie.

Bruce and Karen, you are terrific parents. I remember the first day that you brought Sarah and Julie to school to register them. I knew from your questions and from your responses to what you saw at our school that education was clearly a priority for your family. You have been supportive of our school program and have participated in the life of the school. Thank you!

The story is told of Charles de Gaulle, whose son was born with many serious medical problems. His little life was characterized by one medical procedure after another, and he died at a very young age. The story goes that de Gaulle was with his son when he died, and when the end came, he leaned over and whispered into the boy's ear, "Now you are like all the other little boys." That story came to mind when I heard on Friday that we had lost Julie. For Julie the tubes are gone, the tests, the blood work, the medication, the hospital gowns. She is free now of the pain and the discomfort that characterized the last 3 months. She is whole again.

Our school will deeply miss Julie. We will miss the spunky, feisty kid with the messy desk and the compassionate heart. Karen, Bruce, Sarah, David, our school community extends to you our deepest, sincerest sympathy.

NOTES

1. Blaydes, J. *The Educator's Book of Quotes*, p. 147. Copyright 2003 by Corwin Press, Inc. Reprinted by Permission of Corwin Press, Inc. A Sage Publications Company.

2. These steps, along with other useful information on crisis management, are available from Hubert and Town (1997).

3. This authentic reflection was shared by Steve Mayer, principal at Grover Middle School in West-Windsor-Plainsboro, New Jersey. It is used with his permission.

4. Richmond, Nancy (2002) "The Reflective Principal: Playing With Three Strings" *Principal Magazine* (NAESP). Used with permission.

8

THROWING OUT THE
COOKIE CUTTER: RESPECTING AND
VALUING DIFFERENCES

Human beings, like plants, grow in the soil of acceptance, not in the atmosphere of rejection.—John Powell[1]

LEADERSHIP LINK 8

School leaders model respect for diverse backgrounds and perspectives. They acknowledge that diversity enriches the life of the school. Creating a climate that moves beyond tolerance to acceptance is the goal of the effective school leader.

THE STORY

Two Good Friends, by Judy Delton*

Duck and Bear are good friends. However, Duck and Bear are very different. Yes, they look different . . . Duck has white feathers, wings, and a yellow beak while Bear has brown fur, big clawed paws, and a wet

---

*The story and the quotes in this chapter are from the following book: *Two Good Friends*, by Judy Delton. 1974. Copyright Crown Publishers, Inc. New York, New York. Permission was granted by Julie Delton, Trustee for the Judy Delton Family Trust.

black nose. But they are different in other ways also. Duck is very neat and orderly. He keeps his house clean and tidy. Bear, on the other hand, is very, very messy. What Bear loves to do most is bake delicious muffins and brownies. His messy kitchen doesn't even bother him!

When Bear comes to visit Duck, Duck has to ask him to wipe his feet and not drop crumbs on his clean carpet. When Duck visits Bear, his duck feet stick to the kitchen floor!

One day when Bear came to visit Duck he asked, "Do you have anything good to eat?" Duck explained that he had spent his day cleaning the house and hadn't had time to bake. When Duck visited Bear he asked why the kitchen was so messy. Bear answered that he was busy baking all day and didn't have time to clean.

The next day something special happened to Duck and Bear. Duck decided to go secretly to Bear's house and clean it. Bear decided to bake some very special raspberry muffins and take them as a surprise to Duck's house. Bear was shocked when he walked into his clean and tidy house. Duck was pleased to come home and find the delicious muffins waiting for him.

The houses were clean and the baking was done and so Duck and Bear sat down and put together a puzzle. Two very different good friends found a way to help each other!

LESSONS LEARNED

What is it to respect and value differences? And why is this concept critical to successful school leadership? What comes to mind when we hear the word *diversity*? *Cultural diversity*? *Ethnic diversity*? *Gender differences*? *Differences in learning styles*? *Economic differences*?

In a school setting, students, staff, and parents represent diverse backgrounds, have diverse needs, and require different strategies for assuring their success. The concept of diversity often brings to mind cultural and ethnic differences; however, this chapter explores the concept more broadly. Our conversation around diversity and differences touches on the importance of perceiving the needs and concerns of others, respecting that people learn in different ways, acknowledging that gender may affect learning, recognizing multicultural differences, and relating to people of varying backgrounds and dispositions.

The National Policy Board for Educational Administration published *Principals for Our Changing Schools: Knowledge and Skill Base* (Thomson, 1993), in which the significance of interpersonal connections in schools is explored. The ability to be sensitive to diverse populations is seen as a critical dimension in the selection of school principals. Conversely, it is the inability to work with people and the failure to demonstrate sensitivity that derail school principals, rather than their inability to master technical skills.

The Center for Creative Leadership (2004), a pioneer in using 360-degree feedback to enhance leadership development, developed a self-assessment tool, 360 by Design. Of the 99 research-grounded competencies available for feedback, the following 3 competencies detail the critical role of sensitivity to diversity in effective leadership:

- *Differences matter:* Demonstrates a respect for varying backgrounds and perspectives.
- *Leveraging differences:* Works effectively with people who differ in race, gender, culture, age, or background; leverages the unique talents of others to enhance organizational effectiveness.
- *Valuing diversity:* Avoids prejudging or making assumptions when dealing with others who differ by gender, race, or culture.

In the quest to develop and act on a clear sensitivity to the differences among the members of the school family, what are the lessons that principals can learn from our two good friends Duck and Bear?

Lesson 1: Different Strokes for Different Folks— Acknowledging Diversity

Duck was admiring his clean rooms when he heard a knock on the door. It was Bear. "Come in," said Duck, "but first wipe your feet on the mat." . . . He reached into his pocket and took out two brownies. "Bear, you are spilling crumbs on my floor!"

Bear and Duck were different in many ways. Duck was troubled by Bear's messiness and lack of manners. Bear put his feet up on Duck's clean table and dropped crumbs on Duck's shiny floor. Duck began to run around cleaning up after Bear, putting down newspaper to catch the crumbs that Bear was dropping. On the surface, these two had no chance of developing a meaningful relationship.

How often do we look only at the differences in people? How often do schools try to put all students into a cookie-cutter process and expect that everyone will learn at the same pace and in the same way . . . and that they will all turn out the same? How often do the students who are different slip through the cracks and never reach their potential? How many of these students just drift away without anyone really noticing the special gifts that they can bring to the life of the school?

The wise school leader looks through the lens of acceptance and sees the rich potential in valuing the differences in people, celebrating those differences, and using those differences to enrich the school community.

A Principal Reflects

The first year that I was a principal we had a new student enroll for eighth grade. What made Robbie different was that when he was 3 years old, he had been the victim of a terrible fire in his family's home. Robby carried with him scars over 80% of his body. His face was covered with thick scar tissue; his left ear was gone; and his left arm was missing below the elbow. His appearance made him very different from the other students. I wondered how Robbie would ever fit in.

At first, our students had trouble not staring at the terrible scars on Robbie's face and arms. Because Robbie had told us that he would be happy to talk about his disfigurement, we encouraged students to ask him about what had happened to him and how it felt to be so different. We stood by and watched and listened as our eighth graders got to know Robbie.

We witnessed the growth of a beautiful relationship between Robbie and his new classmates. The result of the open communication with Robbie was that fear and discomfort disappeared. By December, Robbie had many friends. He seemed comfortable in our school.

My most poignant memory of Robbie is from our annual eighth-grade trip to Washington, DC. As our group walked around the streets of the District of Columbia, our students noticed how many people were staring—stopping and staring at their friend. And so these eighth graders surrounded him as they walked through the streets, to protect him from the stares and comments. They wrapped a cocoon of kindness around their friend.

We all learned a great deal from Robbie that year. We learned that open communication was a powerful way to help us find out who Robbie was so that we did not have to know him just for what we saw on the surface.

Lesson 2: Nut Pie and a Messy House— Tolerating Differences

"I must say, Bear, you are a terrible housekeeper but your nut pie is the best I have ever tasted."

Duck decided to tolerate Bear's messiness. After all, Bear makes a great nut pie, the best that Duck has ever tasted. Duck worked hard at tolerating the messiness that was abhorrent to him. But is tolerance our goal? Will we be able to move our schools forward if we seek only to tolerate the people, tolerate the differences that characterize members of the school family?

To tolerate is to suffer or endure, to put up with something, to bear with something. In a school setting, it is critical for each person—each student, each teacher, each family—to feel a genuine sense of belonging. In a 1998 study of why parents chose to remove their children from a traditional public school and enroll them in a charter school, 90% of the respondents listed "feeling welcome in the school" as the source of their greatest satisfaction with the charter school. Many reported that they did not feel welcome in the larger, traditional public school (Richmond, 1999). School leaders who are committed to creating conditions that foster learning must value a culture of acceptance, not one merely of tolerance.

A Principal Reflects

I will long remember the day when I learned the difference between tolerance and acceptance. Jason Jones and his father visited our school and asked to speak to me about the school and the process for enrolling a new student. Jason and his mother would be moving to our town; his father would continue to live in a nearby town. As the details of the divorce settlement and custody arrangements were being finalized, Mr. Jones wanted to learn more about the school. I described the curriculum, reflected on how well our students perform on standardized tests, and provided a snapshot of a school that enjoys a highly positive climate for learning.

Mr. Jones seemed pleased with what he heard but appeared to have some concerns. Finally, he came right out with it, "How many African American students are in the third grade this year?" It was a fair question, one that I could answer without even checking our records. "Jason would be one of three African American students in third grade this year." "And how many third graders are enrolled this year?" continued Mr. Jones. "We have 103 third-grade students this year, and 2 of them are African American. Jason would be the 3rd."

Our conversation continued as Mr. Jones explained that the school that Jason currently attended had a much more diverse student body and that he was concerned that Jason would be uncomfortable, would not fit in within our school. "All during my school years, I was the only Black kid in my class. You know what happens? When Black kids are put in a White culture, folks tolerate you; they tolerate that you are different; they go through the motions and try to include you. But I want more for Jason. I want Jason to be accepted."

Lesson 3: I Must Be in the Wrong House— Finding Common Ground

When Bear walked into his house, he was surprised. "I must be in the wrong house," he thought. His feet did not stick to the floor.

The dishes were washed and on the shelf. He did not see his name where he had written it in the flour on the table. Instead he saw a note: "From Duck."

"Thank you for the muffins," said Duck. "I was so surprised. And it's not even my birthday."

"And I have never seen my house so clean," said Bear. "I was surprised too."

"We really are good friends," said Duck.

Duck had been tolerating Bear's messiness. He tried to compensate for the mess that Bear always made. But he did not truly accept Bear until he acted on his decision to love Bear as he was, not try to change him, not pass judgment on him but accept him just the way that he was.

To accept is to respond affirmatively to someone, to see that person as sufficient. When we tolerate a person, we try to adjust to that person's differences; when we accept a person, we see that person as being sufficient in the way that he or she is. How does this apply to the school setting?

Possibly the most critical application of acceptance in a school setting is how the teachers view and accept or reject each student. Do they see and value only the qualities and characteristics that make students like the other students? Do they accept only the students who fit the mold, conform to the norm? Teachers know that a typical class presents itself as a fairly well-balanced bell curve: Most of the students fall in the average range; some perform at a level that is above average; and some function below level. Teachers are prepared for that and learn to differentiate instruction to the extent that most of the students will meet with success. But how about the student who departs significantly from the normal range of performance? How about the student who is so bright that routine class work is not meaningful or appropriate? How about the student who so struggles with the academic program as to require individualized assistance to make any progress at all? It is in meeting the needs and challenges of these different students that teaching truly occurs.

From the school principal's perspective, a teacher's ability to accept all children as they are and take them from that point forward is a critical quality for an effective teacher. Principals know which teachers are up for the challenge of accepting each student: "I always know that no matter what student I put into Claire's class, that student will be cared for and will learn."

At another level, principals need to be accepting of their faculty and staff members. Is it effective to bring into the school only those teachers who are like everyone else, or is there value in assembling a faculty that is diverse in their thinking, their actions, and the way that they present themselves?

A Principal Reflects

After being a principal for several years, I began to understand the value of achieving a balance in the teaching styles of my faculty. My goal was to have something for everyone on each grade level. Some kids do better in a structured setting with clear routines, defined procedures, little noise, and minimal physical movement about the classroom. Others need a teacher who is okay with the idea that some kids need to do their work standing up or moving around the room. I was learning that if I placed the child who needed to stand up and move around to do his work with a teacher who needed a quiet classroom environment, that teacher would never really accept that student. It would just not be a good match.

In their book *Changing Lives Through the Principalship*, Quaglia and Quay (2003) addressed the importance of belonging for members of a school community:

> The condition of Belonging means that a person is a valued member of a community, while still maintaining his or her individuality. It is a relationship between two or more individuals characterized by a sense of connection and support. Belonging creates an atmosphere that welcomes and connects all staff to the school, including the work they do and the people with whom they interact. A sense of belonging is a necessary condition for a person's sense of well-bring and social engagement. The experience of belonging is also essential to viewing oneself as competent and able. (p. 7)

Acceptance of students, of teachers, a sense of belonging—the goal of an inclusive school leader.

A Final Lesson: We Really Are Good Friends— Diversity Enriches Our Lives

"We really are good friends," said Duck.
"Yes!" cried Bear. "Let's celebrate! Come in and have some cookies."
"But first," added Bear, "wipe your feet on the mat."

Duck and Bear made it through the maze of dismay at their differences to a point where they recognized their commonalities, not just their differences. And now, with good reason, it was time for a celebration.

From shock at the diversity, to tolerance, to acceptance, and finally to finding common ground—this is the journey that leads to an inclusive learning environment. The journey begins with all eyes on the principal, whose responsibility it is to set a tone of acceptance and model for others what acceptance looks like and sounds like. The journey involves ensuring that each member of the school community feels accepted. A person who does not have a sense of acceptance cannot be expected to accept others. When teachers feel that they contribute to the mission of the school, when they feel accepted and valued then, only then will they be capable of extending this feeling to their students. When parents feel welcome in the school and valued as members of the team dedicated to educating their children, then and only then will they support the work of the school.

This is an ongoing process, as schools continuously work to achieve the goal of an accepting learning environment. Remember, just as Duck and Bear celebrated their accepting friendship, it is important to celebrate progress toward acceptance.

CONNECTING TO THE LEADERSHIP STANDARDS: A CASE STUDY—ACCEPTING DIVERSITY AT LINCOLN HIGH SCHOOL

For the first time in the 15-year history of Lincoln High School, a number of students from Pakistan are enrolling. The principal acknowledges that his school has some work to do to create an accepting environment for these students and their families.

Standard 4

A school administrator is an educational leader who promotes the success of all students by collaborating with families and community members, responding to diverse community interests and needs, and mobilizing community resources.

Richard Conklin is principal of Lincoln High School, a school of 850 students in a suburban community. Lincoln High School has traditionally had a homogeneous middle-class White population. In the last 12 months, a number of students from Pakistan have been enrolling in the school. Almost immediately the counselors and principal begin to have serious concerns about how these new students will be accepted by the school community. The conversations in the teachers' room include comments such as "I wonder who will get the next one?" and "This place is not what it used to be; we never had kids like this here before." Many of the new students are having difficulty fitting in. They sit alone at lunch and are not being accepted by the other students.

Design a plan of action to address this situation.

- What data should be collected to determine the extent of the problem?
- What process should be implemented to create a tone of acceptance in the school?
- Who will be involved in the planning team?
- What are the timelines for implementation of the plan?

TYING IT TOGETHER

The professional literature has become increasingly filled with comments on the need for school leaders to respect diversity and value differences in members of the school community. Some writers have stated that failing to demonstrate sensitivity to issues of diversity has the potential to derail a school leader.

- The ability to be sensitive to diverse populations is a critical skill for a school principal. As a visible and accessible person in the school community, the principal is in a position to set a tone of acceptance.
- Diversity encompasses cultural, religious, gender, and racial differences. In addition, some students are different because of how they look, how they learn, or how much money their parents make.
- The goal of an inclusive school community is to transform the attitude of teachers, students, and parents—from acknowledging differences to tolerating differences to accepting differences.
- Diversity enriches our lives—individually and collectively.

THE TOOLBOX: ALIKE AND DIFFERENT

At a faculty meeting or an in-service day, engage your teachers in the following activity. If teachers enjoy and benefit from this activity, encourage them to use it with their students.

The purpose of the activity is twofold:

- to help each member of the faculty and staff appreciate the differences in others and
- to help each member of the faculty and staff feel appreciated and accepted by colleagues.

The activity:

- Read Judy Dalton's book *Two Good Friends*.
- Discuss the differences between Duck and Bear.
- Discuss the things that Duck and Bear have in common.
- Distribute the "Alike and Different" worksheet (see Figure 8.1).
- Provide time for the form to be completed.
- Invite faculty and staff members to share what they wrote on their form.

Alike and Different

Something I have in common with most of my colleagues:

Something that makes me different from most of my colleagues:

How I feel about this difference:

Something unique that I respect and admire about one of my colleagues:

Figure 8.1. Alike and Different Worksheet

NOTES

1. Blaydes, J. *The Educator's Book of Quotes,* p. 213. Copyright 2003 by Corwin Press, Inc. Reprinted by Permission of Corwin Press, Inc. A Sage Publications Company.

⑨

WINNING WITH WISDOM

By three methods we may learn wisdom: first, by reflection, which is noblest; second, by imitation, which is easiest; and third, by experience, which is bitterest.—Confucius[1]

LEADERSHIP LINK 9

The wise school leader knows how to uncover subtle nuances in the day-to-day actions and reactions of those with whom they work. The wise leader is more like a musician in a small jazz ensemble rather than a conductor of an orchestra. The wise leader is always asking: What's so? So what? What's next?

THE STORY

Aesop's Fables, by Jerry Pinkney*

Fables conjure up wonderful images by captivating our interest through short, focused narratives. These narratives not only tell a story

---

*Copyright 2000 Chronicle Books. Quotes used with permission from Chronicle Books LLC. Aesop's Fables, by Jerry Pinkney, SeaStar Books, a division of North-South Books, Inc. The narratives are an abbreviated version of the story in Jerry Pinkney's book.

but also carry both overt and subtle lessons that emerge throughout the dialogue between the animal and human characters.

> The true Fable, if it rises to its high requirements, . . . aims at . . . the improvement of human conduct, and yet it so conceals its design under the disguise of fictitious characters, by clothing with speech the animals of the field, the birds of the air, the trees of the wood, or the beasts of the forest, that the reader shall receive advice without perceiving the presence of the adviser.[2]

Throughout the fable, the animals maintain their attributes—the fox is sly; the bull remains strong; and the donkey practices patience. Their natural characteristics support the moral lesson that they are trying to convey to us to enrich our lives. Aesop's fables are cherished tales by young and old alike.

By accounts, Aesop's life was obscure.[3] He was born a slave in the seventh century BC. As the story goes, he was liberated because of his wit. His death was untimely. It reportedly occurred in Delphi at the hands of its citizens. Aesop refused to distribute a large sum of gold to the citizens, because he considered them a covetousness society. The citizens regarded him as a public criminal, and he was executed.[4]

Many of Aesop's fables survived the test of time. They were transmitted orally and then in writing. Although each fable has many versions, their objectives are the same. If leaders ponder these wise tales, they will understand how to go from a good leader to a wise leader.

LESSONS LEARNED

Leaders must have a deep understanding about their profession. They must have the day-to-day skills that are needed to lead and manage. However, wise leaders must begin to uncover subtle nuances in the day-to-day actions and reactions of those with whom they work. It may be easy to identify the leader who is good at buildings, busses, and budgets, but what about those who understand procrastination, prioritizing, and persistence? How do leaders avoid getting bogged down with details that often get in the way of the big idea, understanding what matters and what does not? Do leaders try to please everyone yet seem to please no one? Do they overestimate their own importance when in reality they are no greater than the support that they get from those with whom they work?

It is the lure of wisdom that makes good leaders become great leaders. Wisdom extends its hand to us. Grab on and invite wisdom to walk along side you.

Lesson 1: The Grasshopper and the Ants— Procrastination and Prioritizing

> Summer's the time to play and sing. There's time enough to worry about winter when the first snow falls.

The grasshopper looked puzzled while she watched the busy ants putting away their seeds and grain during the hot summer months. They were preparing for the long winter that lies ahead. As the ants worked diligently, the grasshopper spent his days making music. He thought there would be time to gather his food when the first snow of winter arrived.

As the snow began to fall, the grasshopper began to scamper here and there to gather food so that he could survive the long, dark, cold months ahead. However, he could not find any food. When he begged the ants to give him some of their food that they had stored away during the long, hot summer months, they told him no. "We worked and you played," said the ants.

Procrastination is a characteristic of convenience that allows us to put off today what we can do tomorrow. Think of all the times when you said that it could be done later, tomorrow, next week, or next month. Wise leaders know what to do and when to do it. Knowing this, they are led away from the most useless of places—the waiting place: waiting for the buses to come, for the tests to be finished, for the parent to call, or simply for the next paycheck. The leader in waiting is the leader who procrastinates.[5]

Leaders know the difference between what is important and urgent and what can wait—what is unimportant or not urgent. The wise leader sets priorities.[6] Know when to wait and when to move on. The wise leader gets things done and celebrates when they are completed.

Leadership is about doing. It is about being a leader now. Effective leaders have time to get things done because they have a not-to-do list. They know that there are some things that they should not be doing.

Think about the difference between leading and managing. The wise leader knows how to get the monkeys off one's back and onto the backs of others, not to avoid work but to nurture self-reliance in others. The wise leader is always creating more leaders.

A Principal Reflects

Harry is the principal of a large suburban high school. He told me about how he did not have time to lead. "There is just too much to do. The day-to-day tasks take up most of my time. Besides, the staff members continue to come into my office with new problems day in and day out. And you want me to lead? Why, I manage all day. Who has time for this leadership stuff?"

I paused and then asked Harry what he does when staff members come into his office and share their concerns with him. "Why, it's simple. I solve their problem, and they leave happier than when they arrived."

"Harry, that's your problem," I stated emphatically. "The next time they come in and ask for your advice, reply with a question. Give them an opportunity to think through the challenges they are facing. See if you can get them to figure out some solutions that may work. The wise leader creates new leaders by nurturing self-reliance in others. It's like putting the monkey on their back and getting it off your back. You see, Harry, the more you solve the challenges that others bring to you, the more they will return to you with new things for you to do. Put the problem on their back and then it goes on your not-to-do list. Wisdom is knowing when to give the monkey back and when to keep it. Wise leaders keep a not-to-do list."

Lesson 2: The Tortoise and the Hare—
Pleasantly Persistent Wins the Race

> Before [the hare] could reach the oak tree, the tortoise had already been declared winner by the crowd of cheering bystanders.

No animal could beat the hare, and she continued to brag about her lightening-fast speed. A seemingly unshaken tortoise challenged the hare to a race. The hare thought that this was some kind of joke but agreed to race the tortoise. As the race began, the hare took the lead and, just before the finish line, stopped to rest. Meanwhile, the tortoise continued to move toward the finish line, one step at a time, slowly and steadily. The tortoise eventually passed the hare, who was sound asleep in the comfortable tall green grass. Slowly, the tortoise continued to move toward the finish line. The hare, who was sound asleep, woke up, suddenly realized her imminent defeat, and began to run rapidly toward the finish line. It was too late. The tortoise won the race.

Principals want to get things done in a hurry. After all, they have a full plate. They do not have a lot of time to dance around issues and challenges that come their way. Quick—get to the finish line and begin another race.

Being quick is not always the best way. Sometimes we have to be pleasantly persistent to achieve our goals. Slow and steady wins the race.

Achieving your vision is career-long journey. Change is about holding hands during the transition from the familiar to the new. Professional development cannot be a one-day fix. Curriculum improvement is continuous, and once it is finished, you start over again. Giving up on a student is not an option. Working with a teacher who needs support and encouragement takes more than a few classroom visits. Dropping in and out of meetings sends a message that what is happening is not important. Leading takes time. You cannot win the race with quick starts and long rests. Besides, too many quick starts result in burnout before the race is finished.

A New Principal Reflects

As principal and curriculum coordinator in a small school district, Margaret usually took the lead in setting the pace and winning the race. When she first came to the district, there was no curriculum process. It was more like sitting down with a few teachers and copying the adapted text into the curriculum guide. It was a fast and furious process. Done, over with, move on. She knew that changing the curriculum process would take time, but in a long run her goal was to institutionalize a process that would be lasting and effective.

Margaret began by creating vertical curriculum design teams that included teachers in adjacent grades as well as those who taught special education and enrichment. She included the library/media specialist, too. When the team met, rich conversations took place. As they redesigned the curriculum, the staff members began to see the value of sharing among grade levels. The mission statement was their starting line. The curriculum platform—a statement of beliefs about the district's philosophy— became their road map. The finish line was not the curriculum guide that contained topics, themes, objectives, strategies, and resources. Instead, the race continued. Margaret arranged for teachers to meet throughout the year in what she called *study groups*. These groups provided continuous opportunities for the staff to learn about new ideas related to the curriculum. The teachers led the study groups. Teachers began to support and encourage each other throughout this process.

Margaret believed that the race was never quite finished. When it looked like everything was ending, she would begin again. Curriculum design was a never-ending process. Slow and steady wins the race. Margaret was like the tortoise. She believed that fast and furious was not the way to go when it comes to curriculum development.

One day she entered the room where the team of teachers convened to begin a conversation about revising the curriculum. Joe turned to her and politely said, "Margaret, you have taught us well. We are set to go forward and really don't need you here today." Margaret smiled and, with a pleasantly assertive voice, said, "You got it."

Margaret set the pace, focused on the process more than the product, and eventually lead the staff to understand that curriculum development is ongoing. It's a slow and steady race to an elusive finish line!

Lesson 3: The Donkey's Shadow—
Focus on What Really Matters

> Frightened by the shouting, the donkey took to his heals and ran off across the desert, leaving the two men with no shade to rest in and no beast to ride.

A traveler hired a donkey and his owner to help him cross a desert. The owner agreed to let the traveler sit on the donkey. He would walk alongside as the guide. The traveler decided to stop and rest in the shade of the donkey's shadow to survive the noonday sun. The owner became annoyed and decided that the donkey's shadow belonged to him because the traveler hired the beast and its owner. As the argument heated up, neither remembered to hold on to the donkey's reins. Frightened by all of this, the donkey took off, leaving the men with no shade and no beast.

A wise leader knows the difference between trivial pursuit and tenacious vision. The leader who continually raises the question "So what does it all matter?" will not lose site of the big picture. We can easily get lost in the insignificant details of the moment. We often find ourselves with no beast to ride when the conversation ends.

Wise leaders do not chase around the wrong ideas. Miguel was a principal in a middle school. When he arrived, the school was like a prison. The climate was closed; students were the recipients of consequences more than rewards; and staff walked around with stoic faces. They displayed little emotion except when they got angry with students or each other. Miguel wanted to change all that. He began by putting out fires, taking a lead role with students, and bucking teachers along the way. He paid attention to the details of the day. He even published a staff newsletter that admonished teachers to thank others more frequently in their conversations than what they were used to doing.

Miguel often confronted others in his conversations. He was even argumentative at times. He believed that by stomping out all the brush fires, the climate would become open and healthy. Miguel did not take the time to paint the picture, to create a vision, much less develop a mission statement. He was too concerned with the details. Miguel's motto was *Get it done now!* At the end of his first year as principal, his contract was not renewed. Miguel had no donkey, no shadow to lie under, and no job!

Lesson 4: The Miller, His Son, and Their Donkey—
Pleasing Everyone Pleases No One

> The miller and his son were forced to turn again for home, without the money they had hoped to make, and without the donkey they had before.

As the miller and his son walked with their donkey to the market to sell him, a group of young girls began laughing and making fun of them. On such a hot day, why would both of them walk along side the donkey when one of them could ride? Without hesitating, the miller lifted his son onto the back of the donkey. As they continued their journey, a group of farmers shouted at the son. They insisted that he should walk and that his father should ride the donkey. The son agreed, got off the donkey, and his father mounted up to ride. A short while later, an old woman glanced at them and scolded the father for letting his son walk along side while he rode on the donkey's back. Quickly, the miller lifted his son onto the donkey. Both continued their journey toward the market place. Finally, a wealthy merchant called out to them. "Carry the poor skinny beast," he said. They agreed. They found a pole and slung the donkey from it. They struggled to the market place. As they crossed the bridge outside of town, the crowds of people began to laugh at them. This frightened the donkey. He began to thrash about. The pole cracked and the poor donkey fell into the river. Now there was no donkey and no money to bring home.

Leaders want to be accepted. When they try to please everyone, they usually wind up pleasing no one. The wise leader instead focuses on building the values and believes that shape the culture of the school. The wise leader keeps focused on the school's vision and mission. The wise leader realizes that not everyone will be pleased.

The leader who tries to please everyone is usually a person who places a high priority on relationships but is not necessarily focused on the outcomes that must be achieved. This can create a school that is more like a country club than a learning community. The wise leader creates a climate in which everyone is intent on getting the job done but in which at the same time trusting relationships grow and become stronger. The principal is supportive and maintains high expectations for the staff. Everyone is working toward achieving the goals that will bring the school closer to fulfilling its mission. Achieving the school's vision and mission becomes the priority.

In schools where relationships are weak and outcomes are not achieved, the climate may become impoverished. On the other hand, driving everyone to achieve outcomes and neglecting to build trusting relationships results in authority-compliant roles for leaders.[7]

Lesson 5: The Gnat and the Bull—Who Is Important?

Pardon me, sir. I'll be leaving now, for I've many important things to do.
But I hope my weight has not inconvenienced you terribly.
Why, not at all . . . I never even knew you were there.

As a gnat flew through the meadow, he decided to land on the horn of a grazing bull. When the gnat was ready to leave his guest, he told the bull that he was ready to fly away. He hoped that he did not inconvenience the bull. The bull replied, "Why, not at all. I never even knew you were there."

Leaders are not as important as they may think they are. Just because you hold the title *principal*, do not assume that you are the only leader in the school. Do not let the center of attraction focus on you. Let the light shine on your followers in such a way that they become leaders, too. Everyone is as important as you are—each in one's own way and in one's own time.

Robinson Elementary School is located in a large urban city. Eight hundred students are enrolled in this K–8 school. One principal and two assistant principals are assigned to Robinson Elementary. Within a short span of 5 years, this school had three principals and four assistant principals. All of these school leaders considered themselves important. Despite the rapid turnover of school leaders during these 5 years, the students in Robinson Elementary School made continuous academic progress. The climate was becoming more open than disengaged; student achievement increased; and the staff was collaborative and collegial.

How was all of this happening when the leadership of the school changed so often? Who was behind it?

Robinson Elementary happened to be a professional development school. A nearby university agreed to have a faculty member, Professor Margaret, spend her time at the school. Margaret was at Robinson 2 or 3 days a week leading study groups; teaching a graduate course at the site; holding brown-bag lunches to discuss professional books; and providing videos for the staff that focused on teaching, learning, and assessment. Relationships began to build between the staff and Margaret. Soon Margaret became the unofficial school leader. Her time at Robinson exceeded that of the principals and assistant principals. The principals and assistant principals had no time to anchor their leadership. Like the gnat, their legacy went unnoticed.

Sometimes the designated leader who holds the position of principal is not the real leader. Wise leaders know that transitions take time; that there is no quick fix; and that, if they want to be noticed, they cannot fly on and off the bull's ear too quickly.

Lesson 6: The Mermaid and the Woodcutter—
What You See Is What You Get

"For your dishonesty," she said, "you'll have no ax at all." And then she vanished, leaving the woodcutter's brother poorer than ever. (Pickney, 2000, p. 85)

A woodcutter was chopping down his final tree of the day. Suddenly, his ax slipped and fell into deep water. As the woodcutter lamented his carelessness, a mermaid appeared and offered to help. She dove into the pool of water and reappeared with a golden ax. The wood-cutter said that it was not his ax. She reappeared, this time with a silver ax. Again, the woodcutter said that it was not his ax. Finally, she appeared with the wooden ax! The woodcutter shouted, "That's the one!"

When he returned home, he told this story to his brother. The golden ax was too hard to resist, and his brother decided to run all the way to the same pool of water, throw in his ax, and wait for the mermaid to appear. He wanted to be rich with gold and silver.

The mermaid surfaced with a golden ax. His brother shouted out, "That is my ax." The mermaid knew that this was not true. She let the ax go. Suddenly, the brother had no ax at all. He became poorer than ever.

Leaders must remain true to themselves. For one principal, it all began at the interview. As the young aspiring principal walked into the room to sit before the panel, she paused and looked around. There were 10 people sitting around a U-shaped table waiting for this candidate. About 10 feet away from the interview panel was a table and chair, neatly set up with a pad, pencil, glass, and pitcher of water. This was for the candidate. Cheryl looked around at her audience, smiled, and then proceeded to push the table up close to the panel so that it was touching the large U-shaped arrangement. She graciously sat down, explaining that she would feel more comfortable up close. That is who she was.

The interview concluded in about 45 minutes. Just as it was ending, one of the members of the interview committee asked Cheryl why she pushed the table up close when she entered the room. Cheryl replied,

"I have to feel connected to the people with whom I will be working. Sitting at a distance is not just me. That's not my golden ax."

Cheryl was offered the position as principal. She soon became widely respected. Cheryl was authentic. What you saw is what you got. It was evident to everyone that Cheryl's work was a reflection of her beliefs, day in and day out. She was consistent and respected for her integrity. When Cheryl saw a golden ax that was not hers, she was quick to say so.

A Final Lesson: The Wise Leader

An experienced and intelligent leader may not know what to do in difficult situations. However, the wise leader looks for the answers both inside oneself and from those who surround her. Recall what collective leadership is all about.

Collective wisdom is more powerful than wisdom that is self-centered. Collective wisdom thrives in learning communities that are supported by trusting relationships. Collective wisdom thrives in learning communities that welcome diversity and support risk takers. Collective wisdom thrives in learning communities where everyone values lifelong learning, where the principal and teachers are collegial, and where everyone feels accountable for the success of all students.

In the school that is a learning community, you can hear the jazz ensemble playing its music. The tune reverberates throughout the hallways and in the classrooms. Each of the players knows when to lead and when to improvise, yet everyone follows a score. The school's musical score is its vision and mission. It is the score that everyone follows.[8]

In the jazz ensemble, the lead musician changes. Sometimes the drummer leads. At other times, the trumpet or piano player takes the lead. In the school that is a learning community, the principal leads but knows when to follow and let others take the lead. Sometimes the leader becomes follower, and teachers become leaders. This is what collective leadership is all about.[9]

The wise leader lives in the present while looking back and learning from past experiences. At the same time, the wise leader focuses on the future. Listen for your jazz ensemble. Do you hear it?

CONNECTING TO THE LEADERSHIP STANDARDS: A CASE STUDY—THE RIGHT TO WRITE: UNDERSTANDING THE LARGER CONTEXT

On the last day of the school year, the teachers in this high school discovered that students wrote sexually explicit, vulgar messages in one another's yearbooks. The teachers' action created a divided response from the students and parents.

Standard 6

A school administrator is an educational leader who promotes the success of all students by understanding, responding to, and influencing the larger political, social, economic, legal, and cultural context.

The end of the school year is a happy time for students and teachers at Liberty High School. Students spend the last few hours of the school year eagerly waiting the summer vacation that is fast approaching while they write personal notes to their friends in each other's yearbook. Comments are usually inside jokes and private messages concerning the year's events.

This year, however, was different. As the hours of school dwindled down and teachers and students spent time signing books, the ninth-grade teachers began to notice that some of the yearbooks had profanity written in them. When the teachers examined the books, they found vulgar expressions and sexually explicit messages. It was more widespread than they first thought. Teachers were troubled by comments such as "You're hot" and "Let's do it." Eventually, teachers asked students to go to their lockers to retrieve their yearbooks. Teachers inspected more than 100 yearbooks and confiscated those in which they found offensive comments.

The principal thought that the teachers were genuinely concerned about the students' well-being and took appropriate action. The principal was proud of the teachers for talking to the students and asking to see the books. The superintendent said that the teachers were within their rights when they confiscated the books that contained unacceptable comments.

Most parents were pleased with the teachers' reactions. They thought that no high school student should be exposed to vulgar or obscene language. They supported the teachers' decision.

A handful of students objected. One student said, "I think it was outrageous. It was a violation of the Fourth Amendment. They need a warrant to search our private stuff." A parent who is a lawyer stated that students have a right to free speech, even on school grounds. Searching a students' personal property could be a legal issue.

About 10% of the parents thought that the teachers did not have the right to confiscate the yearbooks. They believed that parents should censor their children's yearbooks. One parent who did not find the writing offensive remarked, "Give me a break—it's the last day of school. It seems to me that this should have been handled by the child's parent." This parent thought that the staff overreacted. She suggested that the parents should have been asked to come in and look through their children's yearbooks.

A few parents who were offended by the writing requested new yearbooks and received them. At the end of the day, the phone continued to ring, and parents on both sides of the issue vented their feelings to the principal.

- When the teachers discovered inappropriate written comments in the yearbooks, should they have confiscated them? Was this solution a violation of the students' rights? How should the principal respond to the parents who were in favor of and who were opposed to the teachers' reaction and solution?
- What are the political, social, and cultural implications that the principal should consider before replying to the parents?

TYING IT TOGETHER

Wise leaders . . .

- do not try to please everyone.
- do not chase around wrong ideas.

- know the difference between trivial pursuit and tenacious vision.
- are pleasantly persistent and in the end achieve their goals.
- are always moving forward, not waiting around for something to happen.
- do not procrastinate.
- live in the present, look back on past experiences, and keep a keen eye on the future—they make the school's vision become a reality.

THE TOOLBOX:
DEVELOPING A CURRICULUM PLATFORM

We believe that it is a mistake to try to create a hasty amalgam of curricular cultures. . . . When content and learning activities are used for multiple but unrelated purposes, they contribute to an ad hoc curriculum that has little significance to learners or teachers. (Windschitl, Mikel, & Joseph, 2000, p. 163)

If we ask principals what they want to spend more time doing, their reply usually includes curriculum development. Curriculum design is a process, and it results in products, the artifacts that we call *guides*, *scopes and sequences*, and *course outlines*. However, the wise principal leads in the development of a curriculum platform first.

First, we have to know where we are going. Our curriculum platform is all about the essential ideas, the shape that curriculum will take in our schools. A curriculum platform is the pathway to successful student outcomes. To achieve all of this, leaders must engage the staff in a series of conversations that focus on each of the following big ideas.

If we are to connect with today's youth, we must understand the challenges that they meet day in and day out. What are the societal issues that affect your students and that, at the same time, have significant implications for education, curriculum planning, and teaching in your school? How actively should your school become in responding to societal issues? What are some of the societal issues in your community that affect your school's curricula and your teaching? Think about your school's required curricula. What provisions are there in the curricula to address the societal issues that are prevalent in your community?

- *What's so?* As a result of your conversations, make a list of the most significant societal issues that affect today's youth.
- *So what?* How relevant is your curriculum within the context of all of this?
- *What's next?* What implications does this have for your anticipated curriculum platform?

Some educators may think of knowledge as predetermined facts that everyone should know; others view knowledge as flexible and fluid—a product of experiences. What do you value and believe about knowledge and knowing? What implications does that have for curriculum design? How do you provide a balance in the curriculum that will provide for individual differences among learners?

- *What's so?* As a result of your conversations, list 10 items that every student should know as she or he graduates from the 12th grade.
- *So what?* How relevant are your choices? Prioritize the top five. How relevant is what you do in your classrooms to all of this?
- *What's next?* What implications does this list have for your curriculum platform?

What does it mean to learn something? For some, the scores on tests become the best indicators of student learning. Unless we gain clarity and consensus about the distinguishing features of productive and unproductive learning, the improvement of schooling and its outcomes is doomed.[10]

- *What's so?* As a result of your conversations, come to consensus on what you mean by *learning*. What is the difference between learning and knowing?
- *So what?* How relevant is what you do in your classrooms to all of this?
- *What's next?* What implications does this have for your curriculum platform?

What is intelligence? In what ways do you measure intelligence? What does it mean to be intelligent? When the tests are over, when the school year ends, what will students remember? Is it all about facts? Perhaps it should be about patterns: patterns of behavior, thinking, and interaction. These patterns make up intellectual character. Educators should be shaping intellectual character (Ritchhart, 2002).

- *What's so?* As a result of your conversations, compare and contrast knowledge, learning, and intellectual character.
- *So what?* How relevant is what you do in your classrooms to all of this?
- *What's next?* What implications does this have for your curriculum platform?

Now reflect on your understanding about the purpose of schooling and education. Revisit your mission statement. What connections do you see between your mission statement and your conversations about the aforementioned questions?

Using a cultural lens, begin to look at curriculum as a series of interwoven dynamics—a transformative set of beliefs, values, and behaviors; a common language; an artistic expression. Look at the context in which it must work. Finally, develop your curriculum platform by responding in teams to each of the following questions. Then come to consensus.

- What is your vision?
- What do you believe about student learning?
- What is the role of teacher?
- How will you approach the disciplines, singularly or integrated?
- What will your classrooms look like?
- Who will plan and develop the curriculum?
- What do you believe about assessment?
- What does this look like in practice?
- How will you know when you get there?[11]

Create one visual representation of your curriculum platform. What does it look like?

Share your platform with the school community. Reach consensus. Over time, the platform should become self-evident throughout the school.

During the development of your curriculum platform, did you experience some disequilibrium? Were you able to break away from your past experiences? Does you platform resemble what is or what can be? Why or why not?

NOTES

1. Blaydes, J. *The Educator's Book of Quotes*, p. 201. Copyright 2003 by Corwin Press, Inc. Reprinted by Permission of Corwin Press, Inc. A Sage Publications Company.

2. Retrieved October 17, 2005, from *Aesop's Fables*, http://www.pacificnet .net/~johnr/cgi/aesop1.cgi?1&selquote on.

3. One might nevertheless answer that the *Life of Aesop* still makes entertaining reading, something that explains that it has been in print for more than 2,000 years (a publication history that rivals that of almost any book). For those interested in the *Life of Aesop*, the most accurate translation is in Lloyd Daly (1961). One can find many variants in traditional collections of fables—so many that Sir Roger L'Estrange complained in the preface to his 1692 version that the *Life of Aesop* had been "dress'd up" in so many different ways that it was impossible to say anything with certainty on the subject (Leo Groarke Wilfrid, Laurier University, February 18, 1998, retrieved October 17, 2005, at http:// www.pacificnet.net/~johnr/cgi/aesop1.cgi?1&LifeofAesoplg1).

4. Leo Groarke Wilfrid, Laurier University, February 18, 1998, retrieved October 17, 2005, at http://www.pacificnet.net/~johnr/cgi/aesop1.cgi?1&Lifeo-fAesoplg1.

5. Dr. Seuss (1990) discussed the waiting game in *Oh, the Places You'll Go*.

6. Stephen R. Covey (1989) discussed the principles of personal management and explained how to put first things first in his book.

7. Dubrin (2006) discussed the *leadership grid*. The grid explains the differences among the four quadrants of task and relationship.

8. This metaphor began with Max DePree (1992) in *Leadership Jazz* and more recently became a focus of discussion in Smith and Ellett's work (2000).

9. The concept of collective leadership is explained by Chirichello (2003).

10. For a more complete perspective about learning, see Sarason (2004).

11. Developing a culture of curriculum is the focus of *The Cultures of Curriculum* (Joseph, Bravmann, Windschitl, Mikel, & Green, 2000). This list is an adaptation of the chart on page 170, which is an excellent graphic organizer that can become a guide in the development of your curriculum platform.

10

LOOKING INTO THE MIRROR: FINDING MY VOICE

Your life is your message. Leadership by example is not only the most pervasive but also the most enduring form of leadership.— Mahatma Gandhi[1]

LEADERSHIP LINK 10

When you look at yourself in the mirror, is the reflection you see the same as what others see? The authentic school leader knows that who she is as person is who she is as leader. Can you accurately paint your self-portrait?

I do not see it. There is nothing to see! But I will not say so. No fool will I be.°

°The quotes in this chapter and the story that follows are from *The Emperor's New Clothes* adapted by Sindy McKay. 1997. Treasure Bay, Inc. Redwood City, California. Used with permission from Treasure Bay, Inc., San Anselmo, California.

THE STORY

The Emperor's New Clothes, Adapted by Sindy McKay
From the Story by Hans Christian Andersen

Many years ago, there lived a handsome and well-dressed emperor. He was so proud of his appearance that he often strutted throughout the kingdom to show off his clothing. As he was strolling along one day, the emperor met two strangers who bragged that they were weavers. They could make clothing so beautiful that some people cannot even see it!

They assured the emperor that he could see the clothing and anyone who did not would be a fool. He was excited and quickly ordered them to make clothing for him. In return, he would pay them in gold.

As the emperor waited for the clothing to be finished, he wondered if he would really be able to see it. And, if he did not, would he be the fool? So he sent his servant to the weavers to take a look. The servant did not see the clothing but, being no fool, he decided that he would not say so. He reported back to the emperor that the new clothing was splendid and would please the emperor. The emperor was encouraged, gave the weavers more gold, and could not wait to get his new garments.

Eventually the emperor began to become impatient and decided to take a journey to see his new clothing. When he arrived at the weavers' home, neither he nor his servants could see anything. Nevertheless, not wanting to be fools, the servants did not admit it.

The emperor, however, believed that he saw the new clothing. He could not wait to share his new look with everyone in his kingdom. He looked in the mirror and, although he was naked, he convinced himself that the clothing fit well. Everyone agreed with him because they did not want to be called a fool. The emperor paraded among his kingdom, strutting down the streets and shouting, "Just look at the crowd! They love what they see!"

Suddenly a voice of a small child called out, "There is nothing to see because there is nothing there! The emperor looks naked to me!"

One by one, the crowd agreed. Soon everyone knew who the town fool really was.

"I am the fool!" said the emperor.

LESSONS LEARNED

Wise leaders create visions that others want to achieve. They develop and nurture trusting relationships and know the importance of working with teams. They nurture the potential in others and are risk takers. They welcome change and know how to make the transition from the familiar to the new. They respond in times of crisis, manage well, and know how to lead others through good times and challenging times. However, to be an effective leader, you must first step back and look at yourself in the mirror. What do you see? Effective leaders know who they are. The reflection they see is what others see. They are no fools!

Leaders know themselves. It is about being you. You must understand who you are. Listen to your inner voice. Seek to grow and become more effective. Keep traveling in quest of your destination. You must become like the artists who can paint their self-portraits. Landscapes do not get in your way.[2]

You cannot paint your self-portrait if you do not know who you are. Look inside out and outside in. Strive to understand yourself, and then live what you believe. Connect with your voice inside; grab the pallet; and begin to paint. Be authentic. Become like the artists who look at themselves from all perspectives to understand who they are—inside out and outside in.

But be cautious. Do not be fooled. Do not think that what you see is what everyone else sees. Your reflection is sometimes a mirage. As you delve deeply inside yourself, you begin to understand why others see what you may not see. The capacity for leadership is rooted from the inside out. The more that you know yourself, the better that you will lead yourself. The person who is able to lead oneself can begin to lead others.

Lesson 1: Mirrors and Windows—Where Do You Look?

Then the emperor turned to his trusted servants and asked what they thought of the color and fit.

Since none of the men were fools, none could admit they saw nothing at all.

So one at a time they remarked:

"It looks very cool."

"The color is right."

"It looks easy to wash."

"And the pants are not tight."

Watch out for the ruts and potholes in the roadway of life, but consider them for a moment. Do not let them blur your vision or affect your self-image. Obstacles are really challenges in disguise. When they get in your way, where do you look—out the window or in the mirror?

Do not be too quick to blame someone else for the rut or pothole. You may have walked on the roadway first. Sure, it is easier to glance out the window and place blame. That is easy enough to do. Leaders are sometimes quick to point the finger, even if it is their fault. Be cautious and remember this: As you point your finger, there are three fingers pointing in your direction; only one finger is pointing at the person whom you are seeking to blame.

The emperor tried to fool himself, but the voice inside him was crying out, "Look at yourself. Are you well dressed or naked?" He chose to ignore the voice. He was not ready to listen. He did not want to understand who he really was. And, if he did, he was not ready to accept what he would see or hear. Consider yourself for a moment. Perhaps you are wearing old clothes or no clothes at all. And, if you are wearing new clothes, they may not look the same to others.

Lesson 2: Leader as Potter—Shaping Your Life

Some cannot see it?

Now how can that be?

Who cannot see it?

I hope it's not me.

How can you begin to shape your life, to be in charge of yourself? Perhaps it is time to become like a potter. Potters take a piece of clay and shape it into a beautiful vase. They determine its shape. They look inside themselves first. They picture what they want to create. The image of the vase in their mind's eye becomes real only through their hands. They are in control.

You must control your destiny. The image that you want to see, the qualities and traits that you want to nurture, are in your hands. Do not be foolish and think that you cannot be in control of who you want to be as person and as leader. When others try to change the shape, listen. Perhaps what they are saying about you is something that you do not yet know about yourself. Allow others the opportunity to reshape the vase as it spins on the wheel, but always use your hands. You are the potter.

Your experiences will shape your life. Life becomes like the potter's wheel as you spin through this journey. Your autobiography shapes your values, your beliefs, and it determines how you lead.

Go back in time and recreate your life's story. Knowing that story will help you understand who you are as person and leader. You are the product of your life's experiences. This is what makes you unique. Who you are is a result of where you have been.

Ah Nee-Benham and Cooper (1999) captured the remarkable spirit of nine women leaders, through their life stories. As their stories are shared, the reader understands why each of these remarkable women leaders transcends the ordinary. As they looked into the mirror, they saw who they really were. Their qualities, characteristics, beliefs, virtues, and purpose as leaders jump out at the reader. Their understanding of their inner selves defined their work. They knew themselves from the inside out, and they let the outside in. Their values shaped their behaviors, their actions, and their reactions. As we listen to the stories of each of these women leaders, we begin to understand how life experiences shape all of us from the inside out.

Your values and beliefs shape your thoughts. Your thinking shapes your behaviors. What you do and what you say become a reflection of who you are. Your transparency gives way to your authenticity. When you look in the mirror, what you see is who you are. The clothes that you see are the same clothes that everyone else sees.

Think about all of this as a backward design. If someone wants to know who you are, that person can watch what you do and listen to what you say. What you do and what you say reflect your thinking. Your thinking is shaped by what you value and believe. If someone wants to know what you value and what you believe, then that person will watch what you do and listen to how you speak. That person will begin to understand who you are as person and leader.

Who is shaping your life? Are you the potter? Begin to live your life's story.

Lesson 3: Leader as Storyteller—
Influencing the Lives of Followers

> One day the emperor met two strangers who claimed to be weavers of the
> very finest cloth. And their story went like this:
>   "We make cloth more beautiful than any you can imagine!" said the
> first. "With a magical quality," said the second with a wink. "For some peo-
> ple have found they cannot even see it!"

Great leaders tell stories. When you tell stories about your vision, what
you value and what you believe, you shape the thinking of your followers. Stories influence others to take the journey with you. Leaders tell
stories about their identity. They tell stories about life's essential questions; stories of struggle and inner conflict; stories about truth, beauty,
and ethical behaviors. Leaders tell stories of their relationships with others. They tell stories that arouse the interest and curiosity in others. Stories build and strengthen relationships with followers. Leaders as story-
tellers develop trusting relationships with their audience.[3]

Leaders attract followers through the stories they tell but only for a brief
time unless the stories are authentic. Remember the emperor. He was not
authentic. He was deceiving himself. He even believed that he could fool
those around him. Yet everyone in his kingdom knew that he was naked.
In the end, a child shouted out the truth that everyone knew.

Leadership is about relationships. Leaders develop influencing relationships between themselves and their followers. Stories help us. Are
you a storyteller?

Lesson 4: Moral Leader—Knowing Yourself

> I know it is true
> At last I can see.
> I have found the town fool.
> And the town fool is—me.

The most powerful force on earth is not your intellect; it is your values—
understanding who you are, knowing your human architecture.[4] Leaders must have the courage to listen to their inner voices and become full
of themselves. When you live what you value and believe, you are authentic. You are a moral leader.[5]

Moral leaders work hard to get things done. At the same time, they have heart. They care about everyone. They care about the custodian whose car broke down last night, the secretary who is ill, the parent who is going through a custody fight, the teacher whose husband lost his job, and the child who is angry or reticent to learn.

Moral leaders are servant leaders. They serve others through respect, caring, and followership. Servant leaders have purpose, and they derive their strength from the shared values of the school community. They understand how to serve others, and they prefer not to be served.[6]

Servant leaders have a deep commitment to purpose. Purposeful leaders can transform a school building into a learning community. They create communities of leaders and learners. Their purpose creates a synergy that allows others to become self-empowered. In all corners of the learning community, teachers lead because they want to, not because someone tells them to. The concept of one leader slowly gives way to many leaders. The moral leader believes in collective leadership.

Authentic leadership is rooted in moral authority, not in positions or titles. Moral leaders are respected because their lives embody their values. When moral leaders look in the mirror, their reflection is clear, bright, and attractive. Everyone recognizes them.

Lesson 5: Recognizing a van Gogh— The Gift of Authentic Leadership

Then the emperor turned to his trusted servants and asked what they thought of the color and fit.

Since none of these men were fools, none could admit they saw nothing at all.

Look at a painting. Do you know the artist? Can you tell a van Gogh from a Picasso? There is something unique about an artist's style.

When people look at you, listen to you, and watch what you do, can they tell who you are? Do you have a unique style? Are you consistent? The leader who values collegiality, for example, respects diverse opinions and speaks about *our school* rather than *my school*, about *our teachers* rather than *my teachers*. Listen to yourself talk. Do you hear what you are saying?

The authentic leader is honest, fair, and trusting. Authentic leaders build from the inside out—their work is shaped by their core values. Authentic leaders "build their practice outward from their core commitments rather than inward from a management text" (Evans, 1996, p. 193). Authentic leaders have a strong moral purpose.

Lesson 6: The Emperor's Critical Friend—How Am I Doing?

And then the voice said:
"He has nothing on."
"I see nothing! Do you?"
"I see nothing on him."
"What the child says is true."

The child shouted to get the emperor's attention. The child was telling the emperor, "Now that I have your attention, maybe you'll listen to me." The emperor needed a critical friend.

It sounds like an oxymoron. How can someone be our friend and a critic at the same time? Friendships are built on trusting relationships. Critics are honest. A critical friend has a relationship with us that is rooted in trust. Who is your critical friend?

Critical friends guide us through good times and bad times. They uncover our strengths and our weaknesses. Who is your critical friend?

A critical friend can bring out the best in you. A critical friend can sharpen your focus, reshape your vision, and help you listen to your inner voice. A critical friend does not give you answers but suggests alternatives, questions, probes deeply. A critical friend untangles obstacles, fills potholes, and encourages you to take risks as you navigate through uncharted waters. A critical friend helps you achieve unlimited possibilities. Who is your critical friend?

You may be a savvy leader. You can develop budgets, make schedules, plan for a disaster, organize a fund-raiser, and write the agenda for a staff meeting. But are you really in touch with your inner qualities and values? Who is your critical friend?

The professional leadership plan in this chapter's Toolbox section will let you know who you are from the inside out. Let the outside in—get a critical friend.

A Principal Reflects

My wife was a first-grade teacher of 22 years. At her retirement celebration, I read *An Ode to a Terrific Teacher: My Critical Friend.*

It was 37 years ago that my educational career began—a teacher in New
York City.
    At the time I thought I knew it all, was bright and witty.
    "Welcome to CS 50," said Principal Joe.
    "This is a place in which you will grow."
    A permanent sub was my first assignment in the southeast Bronx four
decades ago,
    And, one day, I was asked to take over a fourth-grade class—did you
know?
    For one week I was the sub; then their *real* teacher returned; Miss
Roxby was her name.
    She was quite an expert who was known for her fame.
    I told her all went well and I had a great time.
    The students did okay and even walked the halls in a straight line.
    She invited me into her room that first afternoon back, asked me to
open her desk draws and peek inside.
    And this to you I will confide . . .
    The draws were empty! Miss Roxby grinned and laughed aloud.
    "These fourth graders stole everything from under your nose and you
were proud?"
    I was humbled and realized I was not so bright and witty after all.
    And thereafter Miss Roxby became my mentor and we had a ball.
    Now, 37 years later, I invited that mentor to attend this retirement dinner
To meet an outstanding teacher, a real winner.
    And I would like to take a moment to introduce you to Miss Roxby of
fame
    You see, now she has my name . . .
    Yes, Carol is her real identity, my wife, mentor, and critical friend for 37
years.
    As she ends this part of life's journey, she deserves your cheers!

A Final Lesson: Sculptor, Architect, and Writer

Our story began with a well-dressed emperor whose hunger for new
clothes led him into believing that two weavers could make cloth more

beautiful than he had ever worn. In exchange for a pot of gold, the emperor dons his new outfit and, when he looks into the mirror, sees himself in a suit more brilliant, amazing, dazzling, and indescribable than ever. Yet everyone around him saw a naked emperor, and, none being fools (so they thought), they would not admit what they really saw. It took the voice of a child, the voice of a critical friend, to say that there was nothing to fix, to tear, to see—because the emperor was naked in reality.

Your inner voice is speaking to you. Look at yourself. What do you see? What do others see?

You are the sculptor of your appearance, the architect of your life, and the writer of your own script.

CONNECTING TO THE LEADERSHIP STANDARDS: A CASE STUDY—MS. PERCEPTION AND MR. INDENIAL

The principal denies that there is a problem between his secretary and the teachers. His denial gives others the impression that he is not listening to the teachers' concerns.

Standard 5

A school administrator is an educational leader who promotes the success of all students by acting with integrity, fairness, and in an ethical manner.

Greenwald Elementary is a K–5 school for 310 students. On a typical school day, the office is buzzing with activity. The staff mailboxes and sign-in sheets are in this office. Students, parents, and visitors are in and out all day. The telephone rings constantly. The *ping* from the computer signals that another e-mail has arrived and is awaiting a reply from the secretary.

Ms. Perception is the school secretary. She is also vice president of the professional association.

Mr. InDenial is a well-liked and respected principal. He works long hours. He always arrives before the custodians and leaves long after everyone else has gone home. Mr. InDenial likes everything to be completed correctly. He does many things himself to ensure that this happens. He knows the names of all students and can recognize many of their parents. He welcomes staff, students, and parents without appointments. Mr. InDenial is admired by his staff and the parents. Ms. Perception has been working with Mr. InDenial for 15 years.

During the last 2 years, the staff has grumbled about Ms. Perception's ability to be a team player. Teachers know that the principal is completing jobs left undone by the secretary. Lately, Ms. Perception is quick to reply abruptly to teachers and parents. She recently stormed into the faculty room during lunchtime. She demanded to know whose bottles of soda were in the refrigerator, because they were taking up so much space. Ms. Perception is gossiping lately. She is taking extended lunch breaks but never at her scheduled time. When Ms. Perception is out of the office, the school nurse covers for her. The unpredictable length of time involved in this additional responsibility has made the school nurse upset to say the least.

The situation is escalating, and some of the teachers have decided to talk to the principal about their feelings regarding Ms. Perception's unprofessional conduct. He listened and politely said that he would take care of things. However, nothing has changed. The staff is grumbling, "Why does Ms. Perception get away with this kind of behavior?" Mr. InDenial does not seem to want to deal with it. The teachers are beginning to wonder if Ms. Perception is holding something over him. Is there more than just a professional relationship going on here?

- Mr. InDenial seems to be avoiding the teacher's concerns. How should he respond to the teachers?
- Ms. Perception does not appear to realize the problems that she is causing. How should Mr. InDenial approach this situation with his secretary?
- Is Mr. InDenial acting with integrity, fairness, and in an ethical manner?
- Consider the knowledge, dispositions, and performance indicators for Standard 5 (see Appendix). If you were Mr. InDenial's critical friend, what would you say to him?

TYING IT TOGETHER

- Look in the mirror before you look out the window.
- Shape your life. You are in charge of who you are.

- Influence the thinking of others through the stories you tell.
- Look inside yourself. Begin to know yourself inside out as you let the outside in.
- Seek to serve rather than to be served.
- Be authentic.
- Find a critical friend.

THE TOOLBOX: MY PROFESSIONAL LEADERSHIP PLAN

How do you get to know yourself? You must become a reflective practitioner. You must take the time to develop a professional leadership plan and revise it throughout your career. Your professional leadership plan includes your long- and short-range career goals. It identifies your strengths and areas in need of improvement. Your professional leadership plan is a conversation not only with yourself but also with your critical friend. Take time to listen to your inner voice, and learn how to become authentic. Your professional leadership plan is your road map to success as leader. Questions 1–6 are related to each of the six lessons in this chapter. Answer them and then complete the section My Capacity to Lead. Ask your critical friend to complete the same section. Then sit down and have a conversation. Compare your results.

Complete the remaining sections individually or with your critical friend. When you are finished, look in the mirror. Who do you see?

PROFESSIONAL LEADERSHIP PLAN

1. When obstacles get in my way, do I look out the window to blame others, or do I look in the mirror first? (Lesson 1)
2. Am I ready to shape my life as leader? Am I in charge of myself, or do I let others take charge of me? (Lesson 2)
3. Leaders influence followers by the stories they tell. Do I teach others through stories? Are my stories authentic? (Lesson 3)
4. The moral leader knows oneself. What are my values, beliefs, qualities, attitudes, and habits as person and as leader that I like? Are

my personal and professional values and beliefs the same or different? Do I value knowing myself, and do I listen to my inner voice? (Lesson 4)

5. When others see what I do and listen to what I say, do they recognize who I am? Am I authentic? What don't they see or hear? How will I become more of who I am and less of what I do not want to be? (Lesson 5)

6. Do I realize that I need others to help me find my way? Do I have a critical friend? Do I allow my critical friend to guide me, to help me listen to my inner voice? (Lesson 6)

7. What are some limitations that I place on myself? What can't I do? Why? How can I overcome my limitations and become more effective?

8. If I do not eat yellow bananas, they eventually turn brown and rot; green bananas, on the other hand, continue to ripen. When I look in the mirror, do I perceive myself as being more like a yellow banana or a green banana? Am I too complacent? How can I continue to ripen as person and leader? (Fill out Table 10.1 and reflect on your answers.)

9. What are my short-range personal and career goals? What will I do to achieve these goals?

10. What are my long-range personal and career goals? What will I do to achieve these goals?

Table 10.1.   Strategic Plan for Building Leadership Capacity

Green Here is where I am green …	Growing This is what I will do about it …	Knowing This is how I will know that I have arrived … my banana is beginning to turn yellow!

MY CAPACITY TO LEAD[7]

1—I do not have this trait.
2—I think that I have this trait.
3—Someone told me that I have this trait.
4—More than one person has told me that I have this trait.
5—Several people, including someone who is in a leadership position, have told me that I have this trait.

	1 Infrequently	2	3 Definite	4	5 Very evident
I am (a/an) ...					
Self-confident	1	2	3	4	5
Trustworthy	1	2	3	4	5
Extrovert	1	2	3	4	5
Assertive	1	2	3	4	5
Emotional	1	2	3	4	5
Enthusiastic	1	2	3	4	5
Humorous	1	2	3	4	5
Tolerant	1	2	3	4	5
Passionate	1	2	3	4	5
Adaptable	1	2	3	4	5
Persistent	1	2	3	4	5
Initiator	1	2	3	4	5
Caring	1	2	3	4	5
Risk taker	1	2	3	4	5
Decisive	1	2	3	4	5
Knowledgeable	1	2	3	4	5
Imaginative	1	2	3	4	5
Insightful	1	2	3	4	5
I am skilled at ...					
Planning/organizing	1	2	3	4	5
Sharing leadership with others	1	2	3	4	5
Time management	1	2	3	4	5
Solving problems	1	2	3	4	5
As leader, I (am) ...					
Inspire	1	2	3	4	5
Tell stories	1	2	3	4	5
Energetic	1	2	3	4	5
Build relationships	1	2	3	4	5
Collaborate	1	2	3	4	5
Ethical	1	2	3	4	5
Authentic	1	2	3	4	5
Communicate effectively	1	2	3	4	5
Respect diversity	1	2	3	4	5

MY WHEEL OF LIFE: BALANCED OR UNBALANCED?

Here are some indicators from Patterson (2005) to assess one's level of balance.[8]

- You hear yourself saying that you must make more time for yourself because you are the most meaningful person in your life.
  Infrequently   Regularly   Most of the time
- You must begin to make more time for biking, exercise, running, writing, reading, or any other recreational interest.
  Infrequently   Regularly   Most of the time
- You begin to become more serious and less playful.
  Infrequently   Regularly   Most of the time
- You begin to feel sorry for yourself and do not understand why others do not understand how busy you really are.
  Infrequently   Regularly   Most of the time
- You are an expert at multitasking, and others are amazed at your skill to get things done.
  Infrequently   Regularly   Most of the time
- You listen to others tell of personal joys, but you hope that those "things" are as important as their work.
  Infrequently   Regularly   Most of the time

Here are some reflective questions from Gurvis (2005) that can help us get balance in our lives.[9]

- What percentage of time do you spend at work, as compared to family, recreational, and self-needs?
- How much time do you take each day for yourself?
- What rejuvenates you, and how much time did you spend on becoming recharged?
- Who controls your time? Why?
- How did you get to "ought to do" activities rather than "do" activities?

MY LOG

Keep track of what you do every hour during the day for 1 week. At the end of each day, categorize the items—work, recreation, family, personal, inner self (spiritual)—and use these as labels on each spoke of the wheel (see Figure 10.1). Then chart the proportion of time that you

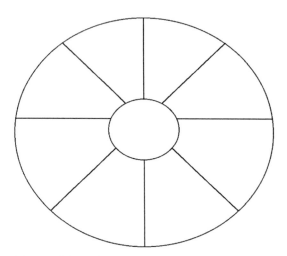

Figure 10.1.   Time Wheel

spend with each category, using the center as zero (*No time at all*) and the circumference as 5 (*Most of my time is spent here*). Connect the dots on each radius. Is your wheel in balance? How can you begin to get more balance in your life?

PERSONAL REFLECTIONS: DISPOSITIONS QUOTIENT— A DEEP LOOK INSIDE YOURSELF[10]

1. I do not feel that this disposition is evident in me.
2. This disposition is infrequently evident in what I do.
3. This disposition is usually evident in what I do.
4. This disposition is usually evident in what I do, and colleagues have told me that they see this disposition in what I do.
5. This disposition is usually evident in what I do; colleagues have told me that they see this disposition in what I do; and at least one person (or more) in a leadership position at my workplace has told me that he or she has seen this disposition in what I do.

As I prepare for a school leadership position . . .
1. I reflect on my personal and professional values.

I	2	3	4	5
No evidence	Emerging	Evident	Evident to others	Distinguished

2. I demonstrate that I believe in a personal and a professional code of ethics at my workplace.

I	2	3	4	5
No evidence	Emerging	Evident	Evident to others	Distinguished

3. I demonstrate values, beliefs, and attitudes in my behaviors that inspire others to high levels of performance.

I	2	3	4	5
No evidence	Emerging	Evident	Evident to others	Distinguished

4. I serve as a role model to others.

I	2	3	4	5
No evidence	Emerging	Evident	Evident to others	Distinguished

5. I accept responsibilities for my position.

I	2	3	4	5
No evidence	Emerging	Evident	Evident to others	Distinguished

6. I consider the impact of my professional/leadership practices on others.

I	2	3	4	5
No evidence	Emerging	Evident	Evident to others	Distinguished

7. I use my influence to enhance educational programs for the good of the team or organization rather than for personal gain.

I	2	3	4	5
No evidence	Emerging	Evident	Evident to others	Distinguished

8. I treat people fairly, equitably, and with dignity and respect.

I	2	3	4	5
No evidence	Emerging	Evident	Evident to others	Distinguished

9. I protect the rights and confidentiality of students and colleagues.

I	2	3	4	5
No evidence	Emerging	Evident	Evident to others	Distinguished

10. I demonstrate appreciation for and sensitivity toward diversity in the school community.

I	2	3	4	5
No evidence	Emerging	Evident	Evident to others	Distinguished

11. I recognize and respect the position that others have in the school community.

I	2	3	4	5
No evidence	Emerging	Evident	Evident to others	Distinguished

12. I examine and consider the prevailing values of the diverse school community.

I	2	3	4	5
No evidence	Emerging	Evident	Evident to others	Distinguished

13. I expect that others in the school community will demonstrate integrity and exercise ethical behaviors.

I	2	3	4	5
No evidence	Emerging	Evident	Evident to others	Distinguished

14. I encourage openness and candor with all the stakeholders in our school community.

I	2	3	4	5
No evidence	Emerging	Evident	Evident to others	Distinguished

15. I fulfill my legal and contractual obligations.

I	2	3	4	5
No evidence	Emerging	Evident	Evident to others	Distinguished

16. I apply laws and procedures fairly, wisely, and considerately.

I	2	3	4	5
No evidence	Emerging	Evident	Evident to others	Distinguished

Indicate the number of items that were referenced by each indicator (see Table 10.2). Use the values to assess your dispositions quotient. Do

Table 10.2.   Dispositions Quotient

Descriptor	No evidence	Emerging	Evident	Evident to others	Distinguished
A: Number of replies in this descriptor					
B: Value	1	2	3	4	5
A × B					

this at least once a year. Compare the results each time to the prior dispositions quotient and the individual items to assess your growth.

Total:

Reflective comments:

NOTES

1. Blaydes, J. *The Educator's Book of Quotes*, p. 106. Copyright 2003 by Corwin Press, Inc. Reprinted by Permission of Corwin Press, Inc. A Sage Publications Company.

2. Kouzes and Posner (2001) discussed self-development and finding a voice as artist.

3. Gardner (1995) wrote about the importance of the leader as storyteller.

4. Paul Wieand (2001), founder of the Center for Advanced Emotional Intelligence, discussed the importance of obsessing about one's human architecture and knowing who one is.

5. Sergiovanni (1992) developed the concept of and understanding about the importance of moral leadership.

6. Sergiovanni (2000) discussed leadership as stewardship. He explained how to become a servant leader with a sense of purpose.

7. Traits included in My Capacity to Lead are listed by many authors and are similar in most respects—for example, see Dubrin (2001). Another source for educational leadership and professional growth is available at http://www.schoolofed.nova.edu/edl/secure/mats/manualela.pdf. *Educational Leadership Appraisal: A Program for Professional Growth*, by Allan Ellis, Ed.D. Copyright by Nova Southeastern University, North Miami Beach, Florida.

8. Adapted with permission from *Finding Your Balance*. Copyright Center for Creative Leadership, 2005.

9. Adapted with permission from *Finding Your Balance*. Copyright Center for Creative Leadership, 2005.

10. This self-assessment survey was developed from the knowledge, dispositions, and performance indicators that are referenced in Standard 5 (Appendix).

Appendix

THE STANDARDS FOR
SCHOOL LEADERS

In 1994, the National Policy Board for Educational Administration (NPBEA) created the Interstate School Leaders Licensure Consortium (ISLLC) to develop standards for school leaders. In 1996, the standards were adapted by the NPBEA and published by the Council of Chief State School Officers (CCSSO). In 2002, the Educational Leaders Constituent Council (ELCC) developed Standards for Advanced Programs in Educational Leadership. They were adopted by the National Council for Accreditation of Teacher Education (NCATE) and are used to evaluate preparation programs for educational administrators in the university/college preparation programs. Recently, the CCSSO formed the Interstate Consortium of School Leadership (ICSL). The ICSL is working with the NPBEA to revise the ISLLC and ELCC Standards (Sanders & Simpson, 2006).

The seven ELCC standards incorporated the six ISLLC standards. The ELCC added a seventh standard that focuses on field experiences for those in leadership preparation programs.

These new standards for the preparation and development of school principals were created jointly by the National Council for the Accreditation of Teacher Education (NCATE) and the Interstate School Leaders Licensure

Consortium (ISLLC). These standards, known as the Educational Leadership Constituent Council Standards, are of critical importance in creating, nurturing, and sustaining a culture and climate that values the soul of the school within its political, social, economic, legal, and cultural context. (Wilmore, 2002, p. xi)

These standards acknowledge the changing role of school leaders. Each case in this book references one of the ISLLC standards. The National Policy Board for Educational Administration oversees accreditation for leadership programs using the Educational Leadership Constituent Council standards.

STANDARDS FOR SCHOOL LEADERS

Educational Leadership Constituent Council, available online at www .npbea.org/ELCC/ELCCStandards%20_5-02.pdf

Interstate School Leaders Licensure Consortium, available online at www .ccsso.org/content/pdfs/icllcstd.pdf

Table A.1. Standard 1: A school administrator is an educational leader who promotes the success of all students by facilitating the development, articulation, implementation, and stewardship of a vision of learning that is shared and supported by the school community.

Knowledge

The administrator has knowledge and understanding of
- learning goals in a pluralistic society
- the principles of developing and implementing strategic plans
- systems theory
- information sources, data collection, and data analysis strategies
- effective communication
- effective consensus-building and negotiation skills

Dispositions

The administrator believes in, values, and is committed to
- the educability of all
- a school vision of high standards of learning
- continuous school improvement
- the inclusion of all members of the school community
- ensuring that students have the knowledge, skills, and values needed to become successful adults
- a willingness to continuously examine one's own assumptions, beliefs, and practices
- doing the work required for high levels of personal and organization performance

Performances

The administrator facilitates processes and engages in activities ensuring that
- the vision and mission of the school are effectively communicated to staff, parents, students, and community members
- the vision and mission are communicated through the use of symbols, ceremonies, stories, and similar activities
- the core beliefs of the school vision are modeled for all stakeholders
- the vision is developed with and among stakeholders
- the contributions of school community members to the realization of the vision are recognized and celebrated
- progress toward the vision and mission is communicated to all stakeholders
- the school community is involved in school improvement efforts
- the vision shapes the educational programs, plans, and actions
- an implementation plan is developed in which objectives and strategies to achieve the vision and goals are clearly articulated
- assessment data related to student learning are used to develop the school vision and goals
- relevant demographic data pertaining to students and their families are used in developing the school mission and goals
- barriers to achieving the vision are identified, clarified, and addressed
- needed resources are sought and obtained to support the implementation of the school mission and goals
- existing resources are used in support of the school vision and goals
- the vision, mission, and implementation plans are regularly monitored, evaluated, and revised

Table A.2.   Standard 2: A school administrator is an educational leader who promotes the success for all students by advocating, nurturing, and sustaining a school culture and instructional program conducive to student learning and staff professional growth.

Knowledge

The administrator has knowledge and understanding of
- student growth and development
- applied learning theories
- applied motivational theories
- curriculum design, implementation, evaluation, and refinement
- principles of effective instruction
- measurement, evaluation, and assessment strategies
- diversity and its meaning for educational programs
- adult learning and professional development models
- the change process for systems, organizations, and individuals
- the role of technology in promoting student learning and professional growth
- school cultures

Dispositions

The administrator believes in, values, and is committed to
- student learning as the fundamental purpose of schooling
- the proposition that all students can learn
- the variety of ways in which students can learn
- lifelong learning for self and others
- professional development as an integral part of school improvement
- the benefits that diversity brings to the school community
- a safe and supportive learning environment
- preparing students to be contributing members of society

Performances

The administrator facilitates processes and engages in activities ensuring that
- all individuals are treated with fairness, dignity, and respect
- professional development promotes a focus on student learning consistent with the school vision and goals
- students and staff feel valued and important
- the responsibilities and contributions of each individual are acknowledged
- barriers to student learning are identified, clarified, and addressed
- diversity is considered in developing learning experiences
- lifelong learning is encouraged and modeled
- there is a culture of high expectations for self, student, and staff performance
- technologies are used in teaching and learning
- student and staff accomplishments are recognized and celebrated
- multiple opportunities to learn are available to all students
- the school is organized and aligned for success
- curricular, co-curricular, and extra-curricular programs are designed, implemented, evaluated, and refined

Performances

- curriculum decisions are based on research, expertise of teachers, and the recommendations of learned societies
- the school culture and climate are assessed on a regular basis
- a variety of sources of information is used to make decisions
- student learning is assessed using a variety of techniques
- multiple sources of information regarding performance are used by staff and students
- a variety of supervisory and evaluation models is employed
- pupil personnel programs are developed to meet the needs of students and their families

Table A.3. Standard 3: A school administrator is an educational leader who promotes the success of all students by ensuring management of the organization, operations, and resources for a safe, efficient, and effective learning environment.

Knowledge

The administrator has knowledge and understanding of
- theories and models of organizations and the principles of organizational development
- operational procedures at the school and district level
- principles and issues relating to school safety and security
- human resources management and development
- principles and issues relating to fiscal operations of school management
- principles and issues relating to school facilities and use of space
- legal issues impacting school operations
- current technologies that support management functions

Dispositions

The administrator believes in, values, and is committed to
- making management decisions to enhance learning and teaching
- taking risks to improve schools
- trusting people and their judgments
- accepting responsibility
- high-quality standards, expectations, and performances
- involving stakeholders in management processes
- a safe environment

Performances

The administrator facilitates processes and engages in activities ensuring that
- knowledge of learning, teaching, and student development is used to inform management decisions
- operational procedures are designed and managed to maximize opportunities for successful learning
- emerging trends are recognized, studied, and applied as appropriate
- operational plans and procedures to achieve the vision and goals of the school are in place
- collective bargaining and other contractual agreements related to the school are effectively managed
- the school plant, equipment, and support systems operate safely, efficiently, and effectively
- time is managed to maximize attainment of organizational goals
- potential problems and opportunities are identified
- problems are confronted and resolved in a timely manner
- financial, human, and material resources are aligned to the goals of schools
- the school acts entrepreneurially to support continuous improvement
- organizational systems are regularly monitored and modified as needed
- stakeholders are involved in decisions affecting schools
- responsibility is shared to maximize ownership and accountability
- effective problem-framing and problem-solving skills are used

- effective conflict resolution skills are used
- effective group-process and consensus-building skills are used
- effective communication skills are used
- a safe, clean, and aesthetically pleasing school environment is created and maintained
- human resource functions support the attainment of school goals
- confidentiality and privacy of school records are maintained

Table A.4.   Standard 4: A school administrator is an educational leader who promotes the success of all students by collaborating with families and community members, responding to diverse community interests and needs, and mobilizing community resources.

Knowledge

The administrator has knowledge and understanding of
- emerging issues and trends that potentially impact the school community
- the conditions and dynamics of the diverse school community
- community resources
- community relations and marketing strategies and processes
- successful models of school, family, business, community, government and higher education partnerships

Dispositions

The administrator believes in, values, and is committed to
- schools operating as an integral part of the larger community
- collaboration and communication with families
- involvement of families and other stakeholders in school decision-making processes
- the proposition that diversity enriches the school
- families as partners in the education of their children
- the proposition that families have the best interests of their children in mind
- resources of the family and community needing to be brought to bear on the education of students
- an informed public

Performances

The administrator facilitates processes and engages in activities ensuring that
- high visibility, active involvement, and communication with the larger community is a priority
- relationships with community leaders are identified and nurtured
- information about family and community concerns, expectations, and needs is used regularly
- there is outreach to different business, religious, political, and service agencies and organizations
- credence is given to individuals and groups whose values and opinions may conflict
- the school and community serve one another as resources
- available community resources are secured to help the school solve problems and achieve goals
- partnerships are established with area businesses, institutions of higher education, and community groups
- to strengthen programs and support school goals
- community youth family services are integrated with school programs
- community stakeholders are treated equitably
- diversity is recognized and valued
- effective media relations are developed and maintained
- a comprehensive program of community relations is established
- public resources and funds are used appropriately and wisely
- community collaboration is modeled for staff
- opportunities for staff to develop collaborative skills are provided

Table A.5.   Standard 5: A school administrator is an educational leader who promotes the success of all students by acting with integrity, fairness, and in an ethical manner.

Knowledge

The administrator has knowledge and understanding of
- the purpose of education and the role of leadership in modern society
- various ethical frameworks and perspectives on ethics
- the values of the diverse school community
- professional codes of ethics
- the philosophy and history of education

Dispositions

The administrator believes in, values, and is committed to
- the ideal of the common good
- the principles in the Bill of Rights
- the right of every student to a free, quality education
- bringing ethical principles to the decision-making process
- subordinating one's own interest to the good of the school community
- accepting the consequences for upholding one's principles and actions
- using the influence of one's office constructively and productively in the service of all students and their families
- development of a caring school community

Performances

The administrator
- examines personal and professional values
- demonstrates a personal and professional code of ethics
- demonstrates values, beliefs, and attitudes that inspire others to higher levels of performance
- serves as a role model
- accepts responsibility for school operations
- considers the impact of one's administrative practices on others
- uses the influence of the office to enhance the educational program rather than for personal gain
- treats people fairly, equitably, and with dignity and respect
- protects the rights and confidentiality of students and staff
- demonstrates appreciation for and sensitivity to the diversity in the school community
- recognizes and respects the legitimate authority of others
- examines and considers the prevailing values of the diverse school community
- expects that others in the school community will demonstrate integrity and exercise ethical behavior
- opens the school to public scrutiny
- fulfills legal and contractual obligations
- applies laws and procedures fairly, wisely, and considerately

Table A.6.   Standard 6: A school administrator is an educational leader who promotes the success of all students by understanding, responding to, and influencing the larger political, social, economic, legal, and cultural context.

Knowledge

The administrator has knowledge and understanding of
- principles of representative governance that undergird the system of American schools
- the role of public education in developing and renewing a democratic society and an economically productive nation
- the law as related to education and schooling
- the political, social, cultural and economic systems and processes that impact schools
- models and strategies of change and conflict resolution as applied to the larger political, social, cultural and economic
- contexts of schooling
- global issues and forces affecting teaching and learning
- the dynamics of policy development and advocacy under our democratic political system
- the importance of diversity and equity in a democratic society

Dispositions

The administrator believes in, values, and is committed to
- education as a key to opportunity and social mobility
- recognizing a variety of ideas, values, and cultures
- importance of a continuing dialogue with other decision makers affecting education
- actively participating in the political and policy-making context in the service of education
- using legal systems to protect student rights and improve student opportunities

Performances

The administrator facilitates processes and engages in activities ensuring that
- the environment in which schools operate is influenced on behalf of students and their families
- communication occurs among the school community concerning trends, issues, and potential changes in the environment in which schools operate
- there is ongoing dialogue with representatives of diverse community groups
- the school community works within the framework of policies, laws, and regulations enacted by local, state, and federal authorities
- public policy is shaped to provide quality education for students
- lines of communication are developed with decision makers outside the school community

REFERENCES

Ah Nee-Benham, M. K. P., & Cooper, J. E. (1999). *Let my spirit soar! Narratives of diverse women in school leadership.* Thousand Oaks, CA: Corwin Press.

Bass, B. M., & Avolio, B. J. (Eds.). (1994). *Improving organizational effectiveness through transformational leadership.* Thousand Oaks, CA: Sage.

Bridges, W. (2003). *Managing transitions: Making the most of change.* Cambridge, MA: Da Capo Press.

Canfield, J., & Hansen, M. K. (1993). *Chicken soup for the soul.* Deerfield Beach, FL: Health Communications.

Carroll, L. (2000). *Alice in Wonderland* (Adapt. Jane Fior). New York: Dorling Kindersley.

Center for Creative Leadership. (2004). *360 by Design facilitators' guide.* Greensboro, NC: Author.

Chang, R. (2000). *The passion plan.* San Francisco: Jossey-Bass.

Chirichello, M. (2003). Reinventing the principalship: From centrist to collective leadership. In F. C. Lunenburg & C. S. Carr (Eds.), *Shaping the future: Policy, partnerships, and emerging perspectives* (pp. 354–376). Lanham, MD: Scarecrow.

Covey, S. (1989). *The 7 habits of highly successful people: Powerful lessons in personal change.* New York: Fireside.

Daly, L. (1961). *Aesop without morals.* New York: Thomas Yoseloff.

DePree, M. (1992). *Leadership jazz.* New York: Dell.

Deutschman, A. (2005, May). Making change. *Fast Company*, pp. 53–62.

Dr. Seuss. (1990). *Oh, the places you'll go!* New York: Random House.

Dubrin, A. J. (2001). *Leadership: Research findings, practice, and skills* (3rd ed.). Boston: Houghton Mifflin.

Dubrin, A. J. (2006). *Leadership: Research findings, practice, and skills* (5th ed.). Boston: Houghton Mifflin.

Duke, D. (2004). *The challenges of educational change.* Boston: Pearson.

Evans, R. (1996). *The human side of school change.* San Francisco: Jossey-Bass.

Gardner, H. (1995). *Leading minds.* New York: Basic Books.

Gardner, H. (2004). *Changing minds: The art and science of changing our own and other people's minds.* Boston: Harvard Business School Press.

Gregerman, A. (2000). *Lessons from the sandbox: Using the 13 gifts of childhood to rediscover the keys to business success.* Chicago: Contemporary Books.

Gross, S. J. (1998). *Staying centered: Curriculum leadership in a turbulent era.* Alexandria, VA: Association for Supervision and Curriculum Development.

Gurvis, J. (2005, January). Take stock with a time inventory. *Finding your balance* [e-newsletter]. Greensboro, NC: Center for Creative Leadership. Retrieved February 20, 2006, from http://www.ccl.org/leadership/enewsletter/2005/JANinventory.aspx?pageId=600

Hall, G. E., & Hord, S. M. (2001). *Implementing change: Patterns, principles, and potholes.* Boston: Allyn and Bacon.

Hamel, G. (2002, December). Innovation now! *Fast Company*, pp. 114–124.

Hammonds, K. H. (2001, June). You can't lead without making sacrifices. *Fast Company*, pp. 106–116.

Hargrove, R. (1998). *Mastering the art of creative collaboration.* New York: McGraw-Hill.

Heifetz, R. A. (1994). *Leadership without easy answers.* Cambridge, MA: Belknap Press.

Herman, S. M. (1994). *The Tao at work: On leading and following.* San Francisco: Jossey-Bass.

Hoy, A. W., & Hoy, W. K. (2003). *Instructional leadership: A learning-centered guide.* Boston: Allyn and Bacon.

Hubert, M., & Town, R. (1997). *Quick reference—A step-by-step guide to crisis management.* Yakima, WA: Association for Supervision and Curriculum Development.

Joseph, P. B., Bravmann, S. L., Widnschitl, M. A., Mikel, E. R., & Green, N. S. (Eds.). (2000). *Cultures of curriculum.* Mahwah, NJ: Earlbaum.

Kouzes, J. M., & Posner, B. Z. (2001). Bringing leadership lessons from the past into the future. In W. Bennis, G. M. Spreitzer, & T. G. Cummings (Eds.), *The future of leadership: Today's top leadership thinkers speak to tomorrow's leaders* (pp. 81–90). San Francisco: Jossey-Bass.

Lawrence-Lightfoot, S. (2000). *Respect: An exploration.* Cambridge, MA: Perseus Books

Lencioni, P. (2002). *The five dysfunctions of a team: A leadership fable.* San Francisco: Jossey-Bass.

Martin, A., McCauley, C., Wilburn, P., Calaro, A., & Ernst, C. (2006). The changing nature of leadership [a CCL report]. Greensboro, NC: Center for Creative Leadership. Retrieved August 21, 2006, from www.ccl.org/leadership/pdf/research/NatureLeadership.pdf

McEwan, E. K. (1997). *Leading your team to excellence: How to make quality decisions.* Thousand Oaks, CA: Corwin Press.

Monroe, L. (2001, March). Take 5: It began 5 years ago. *Fast Company,* p. 98.

Nanus, B. (2003). Where tomorrow begins: Finding the right vision. In *Business leadership* (pp. 351–368). San Francisco: Wiley.

Patterson, G. (2005, January). You know you're out of balance when. . . . *Finding your balance* [e-newsletter]. Greensboro, NC: Center for Creative Leadership. Retrieved February 20, 2006, from www.ccl.org/leadership/enewsletter/2005/JANbalance.aspx?pageId=598

Quaglia, R. J., & Quay, S. E. (2003). *Changing lives through the principalship.* Alexandria, VA: National Association of Elementary School Principals.

Richmond, N. (1999). *Parental choice in selection of a charter school in New Jersey.* New York: Teachers College Columbia University.

Ritchhart, R. (2002). *Intellectual character: What it is, why it matters, and how to get it.* San Francisco: Jossey-Bass.

Sanders, N. M., & Simpson, J. (2006, March). Updating the ISLLC standards for school leaders and the ELCC/NCATE program standards. Washington, DC: The Council of Chief State School Offices. Retrieved August 23, 2006, from www.ccsso.org/content/PDFs/Talking%20Points3.20.06.pdf

Sarason, S. B. (2004). *And what do you mean by learning?* Portsmouth, NH: Heinemann.

Sergiovanni, T. (1992). *Moral leadership: Getting to the heart of school improvement.* San Francisco: Jossey-Bass.

Sergiovanni, T. (2000). Leadership as stewardship: "Who's serving who?" In *The Jossey-Bass reader on educational leadership* (pp. 119–140). San Francisco: Jossey-Bass.

Smith, W., & Ellett, C. D. (2000, April). Timely discussions, but wrong metaphor for school leadership: A response to Brent and Hurley. *Teaching in Educational Administration,* 7(1), 1, 3–5, 7–9.

Thomson, S. D. (Ed.). (1993). *Principals for our changing schools: Knowledge and skill base.* Fairfax, VA: National Policy Board for Educational Administration.

Wheatley, M. (1999). *Leadership and the new science: Discovering order in a chaotic world* (2nd ed.). San Francisco: Berrett-Koehler.

Wheelan, S. A. (1999). *Creating effective teams: A guide for members and leaders.* Thousand Oaks, CA: Sage.

Wieand, P. (2001, March). Looking back: 1996–2001. *Fast Company,* p. 110.

Wilmore, E. L. (2002). *Principal leadership.* Thousand Oaks, CA: Corwin Press.

Windschitl, M. A., Mikel, E. R., & Joseph, P. B. (2000). Reculturing curriculum. In P. B. Joseph, S. L. Bravmann, M. A. Widnschitl, E. R. Mikel, & N. S. Green (Eds.), *Cultures of curriculum* (pp. 161–174). Mahwah, NJ: Earlbaum.

ABOUT THE AUTHORS

Michael Chirichello has spent 39 years in public education in New Jersey, as classroom teacher, assistant principal, principal, district and county superintendent, and professor and chair in the Department of Educational Leadership at William Paterson University in New Jersey. He earned his doctorate from Seton Hall University in 1997.

In his current position, at William Paterson University, he developed a program for aspiring principals and supervisors. In addition to working at the university, Chirichello has published articles and book chapters on leadership and curriculum design. He is a consultant who has presented both nationally and internationally for principals, school board members, and teachers. His work is focused on leadership, change in organizations, team building, curriculum design, action research, professional development schools, and induction programs. His work with school leaders has taken him to Australia, Germany, India, and Egypt.

Chirichello was the recipient of the Educational Leadership Award, from the New Jersey Coalition of Educational Leaders; the Dale Reinhardt Excellence in Education Award, from the Sussex County School Administrators and Supervisors Association; the Distinguished Achievement Award, from the Sussex County New Jersey Education Association;

the Distinguished Dissertation Award, from Seton Hall University; and the PTA Honorary Life Member Award. He was also a Hayes-Fulbright Scholar in Italy.

He is married to Carol, a retired first-grade teacher, and has two daughters: Deborah, who is a member of the New York bar and works in India, and Teri, who is a speech-language therapist in New Jersey.

Chirichello has a passion for developing the next generation of public school principals, and he continues his work at the university and at the international level with aspiring, new, and experienced school leaders.

Nancy Richmond has spent 34 years in public education in New Jersey, as a classroom teacher, reading specialist, assistant principal, and elementary school principal. She earned a doctorate in educational leadership from Teachers College at Columbia University in New York.

In 1998 Richmond was honored by the National Association of Elementary School Principals as New Jersey's National Distinguished Principal. Under her leadership, Mill Lake School received the National Blue Ribbon Award, from the U.S. Department of Education, and the Exemplary Reading Program Award, from the International Reading Association. In 1993 she was named a Dodge Fellow in School Leadership and is a founding member and past president of the Principals Center for the Garden State. She has taught undergraduate students for many years and has been associated with the Program in Teacher Preparation at Princeton University. She has also spoken at state, national, and international conferences for school leaders.

Richmond currently serves as project director for the Principal in Training program at the New Jersey Principals and Supervisors Association. She is a senior associate with the Center for Evidence-Based Education in Princeton, New Jersey, which is engaged in initiatives in Norway, Denmark, Greece, the United Kingdom, and Austria.

She and her husband, Harry, live in Princeton. They have two daughters—Dawn, an attorney, and Suzanne, a certified public accountant—and three granddaughters, Kate, Sara, and Caroline.

Richmond's passion for *tomorrow's principals* provides a focus for her extensive work with aspiring school leaders.